# Early Praise for *Hanlan's Spirit*

After reading Jim Joy's ***"Hanlan's Spirit: Training for Flow"*** I had three initial observations. First I hope that the publisher and Jim spend a little extra money on a durable cover because this book will never be put on a shelf in someone's library. Like a coach's pitch meter and stroke watch this tome will find a home in his or her tool bag. Or like athletes' log books it will always be in their training duffle. Second, I hope the pages are made of sturdy stock with wide margins so the coach or athlete can attach page markers and be able to write pertinent notes near Jim's comments. Finally and most importantly, there is no age, experience or gender requirement to find enormous value in this book. The material within is for anyone who cares about, coaches or practices the rowing motion and the mental, technical, physical and spiritual side of this wonderful activity. Hanlan's Spirit ties together much of Jim's passion about "flow' and "integration". Using Ned Hanlan as the nucleus to which the various elements of sculling revolve, Jim elaborates on every element of the stroke and many of the key approaches to technique and drill development without forgetting to explore the relationships between mind and body.

Hanlan, a Canadian and one of the world's preeminent scullers in the 1880's, sculled on Toronto Island Lagoon, a mostly peaceful body of water separated from Lake Ontario's north shore by a long peninsula of rock. Here Hanlan sculled and thought about how to become a more effective rowing athlete. He encouraged modification to his shell by increasing the track length several times arriving at 26 inches resulting in a more effective leg drive. He discovered how to swing his body like the pendulum on his kitchen clock to maximize the hip and trunk action. He thought about the continuity of the action of the athlete and the shell to create the integration of mind, body, equipment and water resulting in a style of continuous flow between the athlete and the environment. Through miles of strokes and experimentation he formulated a technique and style, which produced world championship results and became the foundation of much of what we see today in crews and scullers on the water.

    Jim Joy is forever our coach, teacher, mentor, choreographer, facilitator and explorer of all that is rowing. He is concerned about the education of coaches and by default the athletes they coach. He believes one can not teach the movements of rowing without understanding the relationships between athlete and coach, sculler and his equipment, and the integration of the environment and the consciousness of those who partake in the activity. The goal of repeatability and effortlessness of the motion to the observer is a key tenet of Jim's thesis. T.S. Eliot, Sir Roger Bannister, Henry David Thoreau, Sir Ernest Shackelton, T.E. Lawrence, Fridtjof Nansen, Zeno Mueller, Carly Geer, Honus Wagner, George "Babe" Ruth, Wayne Gretzky and many others fill the pages when Jim writes about excellence, focus, concentration and being in the moment and not concerned with the past or future. Tai Chi, yoga and meditation are clearly at the root of much of the mental and spiritual preparation not only for the athlete but for also for the coach. The calm and stillness that is part of the presentation is found within the methods, which help prepare the athlete for the learning experience. Jim provides several grids and drawings depicting a seasonal and progressive approach for technical, physical and mental development.

As mentioned above *Hanlan's Spirit* is not a one-timer and then added to the rowing shelf. The genius of the material presented is in its immediate applicability for a coach or athlete. Ned Hanlan's story is inspirational. However, the reader will keep coming back to review Jim's core principles suggesting that technical development is enhanced when the mind and body are ready. Well we are ready and Jim Joy through **Hanlan's Spirit: Training for Flow** has come for all of us.

Larry Gluckman
Former Head Coach at Princeton, Dartmouth, Trinity and for the United States National Team.

# Hanlan's Spirit

# Hanlan's Spirit

## Training for Flow

Jimmy Joy

*Joy of Sculling*

© Copyright 2011. James C. Joy, The Joy of Sculling. All rights reserved.
ISBN: 978-1-257-98863-1

No part of this publication may be reproduced or transmitted in any form or by any means, electronic or mechanical, including photocopying, recording, or any other information storage and retrieval system, without the written permission of the publisher and author.

Published by Nicholas Lee Parker, Agent of The Joy of Sculling

James C. Joy
The Joy of Sculling
P.O. Box 567
Geneva, New York 14456
Phone: (315) 781-2383
Email: joyofsculling@mac.com
Website: www.thejoyofsculling.com

Cover Design by Kit Casey

## Dedication

This book is dedicated to my immigrant parents, James R. Joy and Jane Duncan McKenzie Joy. They were always supportive of my athletic dreams.

## Ned Hanlan

# Table of Contents

Foreword ............................................................. xiii
Introduction ........................................................ xvii
**Ned Hanlan — The First Modern Sculler** .......... 1
**The Flow Phenomenon Explored** ..................... 9
**Meditative Training** ........................................ 19
**Training the Spirit - Mindfulness** .................. 31
**Silence, Stillness, Simplicity** ........................ 37
**Essential Elements** ........................................ 45
**The Rough Phase - Three Major Body Movements** .................................................... 53
**The Smooth Phase - Refinement of the Fragments** ....................................................... 57
    *Release* ............................................................. *59*
    *Recovery* ........................................................... *62*
    *Drive* ................................................................. *68*
    *Entry* ................................................................. *79*
**Summary** ......................................................... 87
    *Postscript* .......................................................... *93*
    *By Way of Thanks* ............................................ *96*
**Bibliography** ................................................... 99

# Foreword

Unlike most of you, I never rowed crew in college and, so far, have never competed in a single on-water race. However, I assure you I am an aspiring sculler through and through. I know this because it is 4:15 am, and my reliable Hudson Sabre (lovingly called Skegosaurus) is on top of my car. Only a non-sculler would consider heading off to practice gliding across a large body of water alone, in total darkness, at such an hour, the height of madness. On the other hand, I am leaving momentarily with my yellow reflective vest.

I am simply a writer who carried passionate dreams about sculling and spent many hours erging before realizing any of them. Over the course of rowing 3 million meters, I read every single book I could find, on both the science and art of sweep rowing and sculling. Following each elite athlete and coach's lineage, stories and reference points led me to the next encouraging story.

In February of this year I attended the Community Rowing Leadership Conference with an air of excitement about meeting a few of the brave men and women whose words had sustained me over the years. I hoped to be inspired and gain some clarity about a possible role for me in the world of rowing. I never expected to connect with a kindred spirit as I found in Jim Joy, let alone become an editor of his groundbreaking new book, *Hanlan's Spirit*.

Upon meeting Jim Joy I experienced an immediate connection and enjoyed our conversations tremendously. The first days after the conference my thoughts returned many times to the concepts of integrated wholeness that were familiar to me from 25 years spent as a social worker.

In Jim's quest for authentic coaching I recognized a compatibility with my own desires to communicate about such thoughts. I sent him an email before fear conspired to change my mind. He responded by sending me an early version of *Hanlan's Spirit*. I was immediately swept up by the spirit of Hanlan's quest. Thus began a volley of words and ideas that has remained the major focal point and touchstone of my days ever since.

After some time and many pages back and forth, Jimmy and I formalized my role as editor for this book. The seasons of this project have served as an apprenticeship of sorts, during which I have strived to find ways to enhance his words without changing either the intent or meaning behind them. Defining the nature of our work together allowed the book to reach a fuller potential.

Since those early days in February, hundreds of hours have been logged in service to that vision. This process has led to a greater understanding of myself not just as a sculler or writer, but as Jimmy and Hanlan continue to remind me, as a more integrated, intuitive, whole.

In June, Jimmy's material began to spring to life when I attended Craftsbury filled with the confidence of beginner's mind and blessed with the capacity to be blissfully unaware of all that was unknown. On the last day of the three-day camp where we practiced in recreational boats, I innocently asked if I could try my single. Discouragement came, along with a dire warning, "if you are going to try out your own boat you had better wear your bathing suit, because you will surely need it." Needless to say, I wish I had been braver but there was no way I would risk being humiliated in front of the race prep group that shared the lake.

The day after rowing school, although determined to get into my own boat unassisted, the fear of doing so was overwhelming. Jimmy patiently reminded me that I had been editing since February and due to that fact, knew far more than I realized about how to row a single. Jimmy helped develop a strategy to not only get me on the water, but do so with safety and confidence. He told me in no uncertain terms that I was not to move up the slide until the instinct to do so became overwhelming. He then assured me it might take many sessions to accomplish that single goal. Jimmy was clearly with me every time I headed off to the lake near my home.

I would hear his voice each time I sat visualizing the stroke cycle before moving too far from the dock. "Remember to do the wiggle waggle, and other drills for your hands. Practice your one arm sculling and maintain a sense of play." With daily practice and many bruises, I soon progressed to the point where I could negotiate the boat onto the car, off of the car, into the water, down and back the length of the lake, with full slide, out of the water, back onto to the car, and into the garage completely unassisted.

Although I continued to progress, I experienced a little glitch when I swam in the lake with my boat in the middle of the summer, not once but twice, due to rookie mis-takes. This led to a few less than pleasant practices. Jim reassuringly confided in me, he himself had a couple of similar experiences. I heeded his advice to continue the practice of shoving off from the dock despite all setbacks.

Working on *Hanlan's Spirit* with Jimmy has been an honor, and privilege. Through the impassioned voice of Jim Joy, I have learned about persistence in pursuit of a dream. I have gained a new awareness of both the art and science of sculling. From Hanlan, the hours I have spent on the water in pursuit of competence have echoed the curiosity and playfulness of his approach. His spirit has inspired me to find solace and answers to some of life's mysteries from lessons acquired while gliding.

Jimmy's tireless attempts to eloquently convey Hanlan's truths have brought a deep humility with the recognition that it will take a lifetime to perfect and truly understand all that sculling offers. It is my sincere hope that you will enjoy reading and grasping these wonderful concepts as much as I have had experimenting with the material found between these pages and engaging with, the man who created them.

May the wisdom of Jim Joy, and the spirit of Hanlan continue to guide this wonderful journey.

Beth Ellen Zwecher
August 2011

# Introduction

Jim Joy's reputation as a coach and insightful Canadian sculling champion first came to my attention in 1971 while I was rowing at Trinity College in Hartford, Connecticut. Head Coach Norm Graf was giving our varsity eight a stern warning the week before our spring race with Wesleyan University, our downstream Middletown rival. "Beware! Coach Joy knows rowing secrets my other rival coaches do not! Joy's approach to rowing and coaching is based on his great success as a Canadian single sculling champion!"

So began my relationship with Jim Joy. In the early part of my coaching career, our paths crossed as opponents. In addition, we both had at different times coached at Yale University. We had friends in common and shared a love of philosophy. Our professional and personal connection grew significantly when I began teaching and coaching at the Craftsbury Sculling Center in 1982. Craftsbury is where I fell in love with the art of single sculling and the subtleties of teaching and coaching. Jim the educator, thinker, athlete and coach became my mentor, friend and confidant. Perhaps fate was working on my behalf. Nonetheless, I am honored to introduce Jim's new book about Ned Hanlan's influence on sculling and the concept of flow.

Jim is the classic philosopher coach in the tradition established by George Pocock. He draws on many years of athletic excellence and personal coaching experience. He also has a vast knowledge of philosophy and literature. Jim's emotional and spiritual investment in the subject of flow is what makes Jim and his story of Ned Hanlan special. Jim's dedication to this subject has been, in different forms, the sole focus of Jim's professional life. Jim's passion to understand and communicate the elements and nature of flow has been, in my opinion, his quest for the sculling equivalent of the 'holy grail.'

    Jim begins his book by describing the rich elements of Ned Hanlan's 19th century worldview. Jim then explains that the way Ned Hanlan experienced and understood the world around him was the foundation of his sculling genius and competitive success.

    Jim's description of Ned Hanlan's life as a sculler and the way Hanlan combined mind, body and spirit to produce a unified experience that flowed has universal appeal. Jim's story inspires and then goes on to enlighten and guide the reader toward attainment of the flow state.

    In subsequent chapters, Jim describes a detailed plan for the aspiring sculler or coach that refines the process that Hanlan used to create what would later become known as flow. Jim is careful to point out that in Hanlan's time the word "flow" was not used to describe Hanlan's seemingly effortless and magical speed. Even today, coaches and athletes may use other terms besides the word flow to describe a sculler or crew that "makes it look easy" or "smooth." The physicist might describe Hanlan's shell as possessing constant velocity. Expert and the uninitiated alike will all agree however, that motion on the water that is choppy, abrupt and uneven is not worthy of imitation and is relatively uncompetitive.

    Jim does a masterful job of capturing the reader's imagination regarding the elusive concept of flow and then methodically creates a detailed plan with drills and anecdotes that both sculler and coach can follow toward the achievement of the flow state. Jim is not just the philosopher but also the pragmatist. He blends theory with practice against the backdrop that states that in the end the experience of flow can only be truly achieved if both the sculler and coach live a life of balance and integration off the water as well as on the water. Jim is also careful to caution the reader that the path toward the flow experience must be approached in a methodical and patient fashion. Although a sculler may stumble into and then out of the flow state, Jim is committed to sharing his knowledge and experience in such a way that the achievement of flow is more easily attainable on a predictable basis. Jim is passionate in his encouragement that the sculler and coach embrace a holistic lifestyle. For Jim, flow on the water can only happen when the athlete or coach are also in the spirit of flow off the water. It is Jim's belief and from my experience I wholeheartedly agree, the experience of flow in the athletic arena is a manifestation of the sculler and coach's life of balance and integration in all other aspects of their lives.

## Jimmy Joy

    Jim has been my unofficial sculling coach for over 20 years. In 1989, Jim introduced me to the concept of "the sculler's catch." Jim discusses this idea near the end of his book under the heading entitled Entry. My journey in pursuit of this concept as a sculler and a coach has been long and challenging. This year, for the first time, I was successful in what I believe to be the effective implementation of the flow concept both with my team and in my own sculling. Jim and I both agree that the attainment of flow on the water depends on a different understanding of the "entry" and "release." This year I was able to experience as a sculler and with my team a smoother running shell that moved with less check due to the implementation of "the sculler's catch." My freshman four that enjoyed competitive success throughout the season and at our New England Championship moved very efficiently and was therefore more competitive not because they were more powerful than the competition, but because the crew slowed down less at the point where their blades went in and out of the water! What was fascinating to realize and Jim confirms my realization in his book, was that changing my approach to the entry and release forced me to rethink my understanding of all the other elements of the rowing and sculling stroke. My realization conforms to a very important and basic premise in Jim's book. All elements of the sculling or rowing stroke are inherently interrelated, when one piece changes, all the other pieces must change as well!

    Jim's book on *Hanlan's Spirit* and its relation to the experience of flow should be seen as an introduction to and not the end of the conversation on the topic of flow. Jim inspires and instructs the reader but also challenges the athlete and coach to become an eclectic student of the subject. Jim's passionate belief that the balanced and well-integrated life off the water sets the stage for the flow experience on the water is similar to Plato's belief that "only the examined life was worth living." Jim's book also reminded me of the quote by the famous English rowing coach, Steve Fairbairn, "a race well rowed is reward in itself." Jim might add that the experience of flow is the <u>reward</u> for living a centered and harmonious life.

Ric Ricci, Head Coach Connecticut College
September 2011

# Ned Hanlan — The First Modern Sculler

Ned Hanlan was a Canadian sculler and World Champion in the 1870's and 1880's. In addition to being a superb competitor and lifelong student of sculling, he was probably the first sculler who performed with flow, making him a true forerunner. He integrated his shell, body, mind and spirit into a dynamic, fluid, unified movement. His stroke proved to be extremely effective, and although he was only 5'8" tall and 155 pounds at his peak, he still easily defeated much larger opponents. Between 1876 and 1886 he won more than 300 races, losing only 6 times. Professional sculling peaked between 1870 and 1900 with Hanlan as its premier star. Professionalism would last another 30 year until it was obliterated by the dominance of the great Australian Bobby Pearce. These two men were the bookends that marked the beginning and ending of this colorful era, with their superb technical sculling.

We can only speculate that the reason for his success against his larger opponents was due almost entirely to his highly efficient stroke and his extensive background in watermanship, which began at an early age. Knowing that he was a highly accomplished technical sculler, what valuable lessons can we learn from this master craftsman?

For one thing, his deep reflection, and the results of his subsequent experimentation, were all refined on this quiet backwater of Toronto harbor. Hanlan, self taught, was able to observe, create, sense and feel his way to an extremely efficient stroke pattern, making him the consummate explorer for new methods and information.

Hanlan was born of Irish immigrants on Toronto Island at Mugg's Landing, near the site of the annual Canada Day's regatta course. A perfect spot for sculling, it provided a haven from the choppy waters of Toronto Harbor and the ideal location for his reflections, observations and experiments with the sculling stroke. The proximity of this watery childhood playground to his home led the youngster to build and row a makeshift shell to the city when he was five years old.

His initial attempt at boat building clearly demonstrated his enthusiasm for the sport and the beginning of a deep, spiritual bond with his shell, oars and water. Frank Cosentino in his little book, *Ned Hanlan*, writes that, "to go to the mainland, Hanlan rowed: for errands, Hanlan rowed: for play, Hanlan rowed. The boat was his servant, playmate, and means of exploration."[1]

It was here on the calm waters of the island's lagoon that he worked daily to hone his technique,

---

[1] Frank Consentino, "Ned Hanlan— Canada's Premier Oarsman: A Case Study in 19th Century Professionalism" (University of Western Ontario, 1974), 8.

skills, endurance and speed. The lesson for the modern sculler who has aspirations is that you have to put in the miles and years of concentrated practice.

This near unparalleled setting worked in consort with his keenly sensitive observant eye for efficient movements to produce a smooth run of the shell. In 1898 he wrote, "I spent months practicing in that direction (the pendulum body swing), and every day I noticed an improvement in my speed. At first it was very awkward; I could not ascertain how to accomplish the object I had in view; when it came across my mind like a flash that the control of the whole motion of the body while in the boat lay in my feet. I ascertained that every time I took a stroke, I threw the whole weight of my body on my feet, thereby causing the stern of the boat to be submerged inordinately in the water. It took considerable time to conquer the habit, but finally accomplished it and by degrees got every muscle of my body working in perfect unison."[2] He was porpoising his shell, but, through careful observation, reflection and change, he was able to achieve a "horizontal stroke".

Hanlan was an imaginative and creative innovator who related the external world of the clock to the internal sculling world of the trunk action, that effectively enhanced his sculling. In lengthening the track he was able to modify the swing, making it more subtle and integrated with the legs and arms, as well as more horizontal. It was in sharp contrast to the shorter track and fixed seat rowing of his day that

---

[2] Ned Hanlan, "The Oar," *Vancouver World*, April 12 1898.

would produce in his opponents a more pendular action of the trunk.

He described his own technique during his career as follows: "A full long reach, out over the toes, with both arms straight, and a sharp clean catch of the water. It was a powerful, steady, horizontal stroke, with application of the whole force at the moment of immersion, a clean feather and a low quick recovery, shooting out at the moment of the finish." With Hanlan's modern approach to wholeness and integration, his description of the stroke is worth careful scrutiny.

One observer commented, "Hanlan possessed an efficient technique, and to this day is regarded as one of the greatest scullers of all time. His movements were so smooth, that his boat never appeared to lose speed between strokes. He was an acknowledged master of both the sliding seat and simple execution of the stroke cycle, so that Hanlan's boat moved through the water as if pulled by a string."[3] The gunwales remained level and the boat slid easily and effortlessly through the water.[4] Indeed, he referred to this quality as the horizontal stroke.

Shortly before the end of the 19th century, Hanlan, practicing quietly and protected from the hustle and bustle of a growing Toronto, was able to focus on the development of both his skill and spirit, and concentrative powers. These strengths became obvious in his races. Today, it is a significant challenge for the athlete to train without earphones, TVs, reading materials or music in the gym. However,

---

[3] Thomas J. West, *Ned Hanlan*.

[4] Inspired by Art Wilmarth, Corrospondence on "Sliding" Characteristic of Swimmers.

creating an opportunity to ignore these technological distractions develops the athlete's ability to rely simply on the essential self.

Hanlan combined those rare qualities of spirit, mastery and basic science, demonstrated by his adoption of the sliding seat, his perfection of technique, great athletic ability, profound love of nature and devotion to his island home.

Although the term "flow" was not in common use during Hanlan's time, he was fully committed to a smooth, efficient movement that was supple and subtle for achieving greater length, power and economy. Consequently, he felt that good technical form and posture were especially desirable and these qualities could be gained only by steady concentrated practice.[5] This was the "spirit" of Hanlan, which permeated his training, technique and entire being, creating the ultimate waterman.

Rowing with flow requires the recruitment of individual cells from every part of the body so that the sculler becomes the conductor of an integrated orchestra. Similarly, the synchronization of the major muscle groups with the skeletal and neural systems was exceedingly critical for the small-statured Hanlan. It is the stuff that intrigues the latent scientist and artist in us all. Hanlan was the forerunner to the various great athletes of the 20th Century who performed with flow in their sports. His commitment to an integrated body action is noteworthy.

---

[5] R.F. Kelley, *American Rowing: Its Background and Traditions* (G. P. Putnam's sons, 1932).

Hanlan serves as an excellent example of an athlete who was a keen observer of his own body movements, his internal state and the run of his shell. Old photographs of Hanlan show him sculling beautifully with an erect yet relaxed posture and a totally extended trunk, an overall excellent display of modern athleticism.

The British philosopher Martin Lings' definition of the simple man is an accurate description of Hanlan and his approach to sculling: "the truly simple man is an intense unity: he is complete and wholehearted, not divided against himself."[6] This is an accurate description of Hanlan's mental approach to sculling. For this reason he was one of the few successful self taught scullers in rowing history.

To evaluate the degree of simplicity in ones life as Hanlan appears to have done, we must consider the observations earned both in and out of the shell. Similarly, to reach this standard of excellence any successful athlete has to possess this oneness of body, spirit, emotions, and mind.

To modify, change or have the athlete's technique evolve to a refined level, the physical and mental training programs have to be periodized. For objective planning the sculler requires a skilled and knowledgeable coach. The coach should work from a plan (see Diagram 1- The Periodization of Technique).

Robert Fitzpatrick, an excellent sculling coach, was well aware of the influence of the professionals like Hanlan, Thomas Loudon, Jim Rice and the Ten Eycks. In addition, he studied the technique of English Orthodox school, the sculling of Robert

---

[6] Martin Lings, *Ancient Beliefs & Modern Superstitions*, Revised ed. (London: Archetype, 2001).

Pearce and the coaching methods of Steve Fairbairn. These influences led to Fitzpatrick's development of a highly eclectic modern stroke that was effective over his coaching lifetime and beyond. He had a simple teaching procedure organized from large muscle groups to smaller, creating a whole-part-whole coaching approach.

Fitzpatrick started with the release phase, then went to the trunk swing for the recovery and drive. The skill of the release established early would insure stability out of the bow. With the drilling on the swing he was trying to achieve the early connection between the shell and the body. The simulation exercises over the winter perfected the recovery and drive timing. The blade work and leg work were the last segments to be addressed. The technique plan is simple, but very effective, and should be woven into the fabric of the overall training including the physical and mental dimensions.

The technique training should incorporate the best parts of traditional and modern strategies from old English Orthodoxy to present day Nolte's sequencing theory. This approach recognizes the simple fact that no one can be completely wrong. The writings of Lehmann, Bourne, Fairbairn, Page, Burnell, Herberger, Klavora and Nolte all must be studied. There is value in all these sources at some level and for some stage in the athlete's development.

The book is laid out to parallel the periodization of technique going from the larger muscle action to the smaller, from general to specific, from whole to part, and from rough to refined movements. In keeping with Hanlan's smoothness, power, and simplicity, this book attempts to mirror his flow.

## Diagram 1 - Periodization of Technique[7]

| Sep | Oct | Nov | Dec | Jan | Feb | Mar | Apr | May | Jun | Jul | Aug |
|---|---|---|---|---|---|---|---|---|---|---|---|
| \multicolumn{4}{Prep I} | | | | | | | | | |

| Sep | Oct | Nov | Dec | Jan | Feb | Mar | Apr | May | Jun | Jul | Aug |
|-----|-----|-----|-----|-----|-----|-----|-----|-----|-----|-----|-----|
| Prep I | | | | Prep II | | | | Performance | | | |
| Whole | | | | Parts | | | | Whole | | | |
| General | | | | Specific | | | | General | | | |
| Rough | | | | Smooth | | | | Automatic | | | |
| Release & Follow Through | | | | Trunk/Seat Timing at Entry | | | | Legwork - Drive & Recovery | | | |
| Posture - Trunk/Hands | | | | Posture - Hands/Wrists/Trunk | | | | Posture - Hands/Trunk/Legs | | | |
| Relaxation Quiet sitting | | | | Visusalization Quiet sitting | | | | Concentration/Mindfulness Quiet sitting | | | |

Hanlan illustrates this simplicity with the incomparable effort and efficiency in his approach to sculling. He achieved this qualitative skill just before the 20th century would rapidly usher in quantity, measurement and, most recently for rowing, the ergometer score. For these reasons it is wise to acquaint ourselves with Hanlan's accomplishments. Reflection on the personal qualities and nature of the diminutive Hanlan, as one of the first great spirits and masters of flow in sculling, allows us to use *Hanlan's Spirit* as a barometer for future scullers. Hanlan's flow was a distillation of his many years on the waters of the Center Island lagoon.

---

[7] Periodization is the detailed process covering all aspects of the yearly training program

# The Flow Phenomenon Explored

> *"There is a way of living, not theoretically or intellectually, but actually, a way of life, in which there is no division what so ever; a way of life in which action is not fragmented, so that it is one constant Flow, where every action is related to all other actions."*
> J. Krishnamurti

In sculling flow is the integration of efficient bodywork combined with fluid blade work throughout all phases of the stroke cycle. The resulting pattern is adaptable, reflexive and instinctual. The notion of flow offers a unique level and form of movement. This uncommon quality may not be evident during every practice session, unless the goal is smooth muscle action. Intensity and consistency of attention are required. It is the task of this book to explore this phenomenon in detail, particularly with respect to the sculling pattern.

This is important for the quality of our lives in and out of the shell. It provides a deep-seated awareness and focus to our inner being. We become much more in touch with our immediate environment. "We are a body rather than we have a body."[8] There develops a wholeness and unity in ourselves.

The young athlete can start working on flow off the water by careful attention to posture and in everyday activities such as walking, sitting, driving a car, cutting hedges, washing dishes and a host of other activities. Attention to detail, focus, and concentration in sculling practice is simply an expression of integrity that is carried over into everyday life. It is important to not confine flow simply to your work in the shell.

The five stages of Flow are: slow down and meditate, create a relaxed posture starting with the hands on the handles; establish a consistent stroke length; focus on the three major segments in the cycle (the trunk swing, leg drive, and draw of the arms by concentrating and feeling the movements); refine specific movements (to achieve integration between the body movements, blade work, and movement of the shell); and finally, practice and drill (until the movements are reflexive, intuitive and instinctive).

The mind is trained to be sensitive to the individual body movements, so that they become one with the movement of the shell. This awareness is largely centered in the hands and the hips. The hands monitor the neat, accurate blade entry and the clean, reflexive release. The hips control the accurately-timed trunk action on the recovery, as well as the power of the whole body and blade during the drive phase.

---

[8] Ken Wilber, *The Collected Works of Ken Wilber* (Boston, MA: Shambhala, 1999).

Examples of the "smoothness" that exemplify flow from other sports include the swings of Babe Ruth, Ted Williams, Ichiro Suzuki and Rory McIlroy. The great scullers Pearce, Kelly Sr. and Ivanov, and more recently, Karpinen, Ruchow, Haining and Lange all had this quality in their strokes. It is critical that each fragment of the stroke cycle be performed with a fluid action. This includes the hands at entry and release, steady leg-work and blade pressure on the drive, completed with a subtle closing of the chest to the knees on the recovery.

The rowing literature from the former East Germany recognized flow as an important technique objective when it was stated that, "each stroke must form one unity and all strokes must be blended fluently and harmoniously."

As flow develops from the smooth execution of the individual parts, it carries over into the complete stroke, and continues from practice into races, which is the ultimate goal. It becomes a consolidated, unified reflex. This is a situation where the micro reflects the macro involving meticulous practice and concentration by the athlete and daily observation by the coach.

Moshe Feldenkrais, an expert in the field of movement, stated that athletes must learn to turn strenuous movements into effective, smooth movements. This requires miles and miles of rowing and hours of intensive, meticulous drilling. Al Morrow relates how his Gold Medal Olympic double of Marnie McBean and Kathleen Heddle would spend countless hours over the winter months on Burnaby Lake drilling on the timing at the entry. Through this precise and patient process, athlete, oars, shell and water become one - not fragmented, but whole. There exists an unspoken resolve by the coach and the sculler to see this goal achieved.

It is important to recognize that the current literature on flow by researchers such as Mihaly Cziksentmihalyi views flow as "peak performance." He writes, "we experience it as a unified flowing from one movement to the next in which we feel control of our actions, and in which there is little distinction between the self and environment; between stimulus and response; or between past, present, and future."[9] However, he does not tackle the difficult questions associated with the process whereby flow is achieved. In contrast, this book's approach is to focus on both the external and internal skills to achieve flow as a 'plateau' experience, involving fluid movements of the parts that can be replicated almost daily.

With the careful nourishment of regular practice this efficient motion is afforded the best possible opportunity to blossom into a stable, consistent stroke that provides a sense of effortless speed and sustainable energy. Commitment to smooth movements by both the athlete and coach, lead to flow in the athlete's mind, body, blades and shell. The harmonious coexistence of these four components creates a fluid, seamless, constant stream of action. This action contains a high degree of economy of motion, simplicity and accuracy, producing an effortless rhythm to the stroke. Eventually, mental training nourishes the mind, integrating and paralleling the graceful motions of the body. In this regard, the athlete develops calmness, patience, consistency and persistence.

---

[9] Mihaly Csikszentmihalyi, *Flow: The Psychology of Optimal Experience* (New York, NY: Harper & Row, 1990).

What was missing from Hanlan's training, as well as the training of most modern scullers, is a systematic programming that provides a deeper mental consciousness to accelerate the development of physical qualities and skills. (see The Bridge diagram below). This in turn, makes it more likely for the athlete to have these "Flow" experiences sooner in his rowing life. Hanlan relied solely on his racing experience to gain these skills, and unfortunately this is the case with many young athletes today.

## Diagram 2 - The Bridge from Basics to Refinement

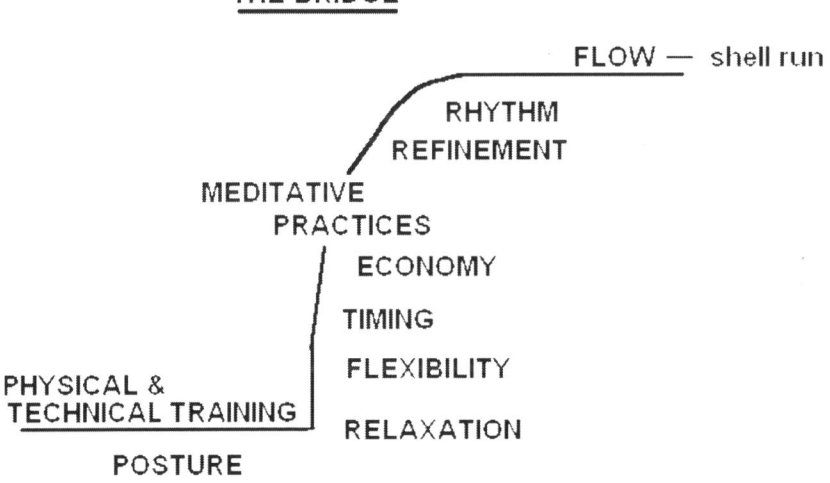

From the outset, flow, in its basic form of fluid movement, is viewed as the primary objective or umbrella for the training including the psychological, physiological, neurological and technical. By emphasizing fluidity as the training objective the following benefits are realized: a focus is established for improvement in the athlete's concentration, skills develop that lead to effortless movement and efficiency in the individual's physiology and stroke mechanics. The cumulative effect of enhancements results in a higher quality in each stroke leading to efficient shell run. Mentally, the athlete is more focused and relaxed. Flow becomes the ingredient that flavors all aspects of training both on and off the water.

When the coach serves as a detail oriented, intensive choreographer in combination with high-level concentration from the athlete, the result is economical movement that is reproducible on a daily basis. Each diligently monitors the technique for smooth action. The athlete is always encouraged to visualize the individual parts simultaneously with the whole stroke as the feel for it is developed and the coach gains an "eye" for this effortless stroke. This development is enhanced by meditation, and by accurate and regular demonstration of the stroke by the coach.

This type of coaching balances analytical, linear thinking with intuitive, holistic and integrative thought. The planning, organization and conduct of the training are analytical and linear; the actual physical training is done with feeling, intuition and wholeness. This approach produces movements that appear to be effortless.

Running, dancing, skating and swimming, like sculling, provide excellent opportunities to observe the athlete striding and gliding. Observations and regular evaluation of the athlete's fine movements also reinforce these principles. It is important for the sculling coach to observe these sports for viewing effective power application during the stride and the relaxation on the recovery or glide phase. It has an appeal to the artist in all of us.

Awareness of integration and rhythm found in other sports is helpful for our coaching. It is also a demonstration of our appreciation of the athleticism displayed in the arts and other sports. I recall how a friend and colleague, Thor Nilsen, took time out from his busy programming with his rowing athletes to view figure skaters in competition. Edgar Degas the 19th Century sculptor was enthralled with the skill, power, and plasticity of the dancer and the thoroughbred. Created during the same period of Degas are the works of Thomas Eakins, who captures the artistry of the sculler. The great English sculler, writer and Olympian F.S. Kelly, was also an excellent pianist.

Throwing and hitting a ball are also excellent examples of a highly coordinated, integrated striding action. Swinging a golf club or baseball bat are excellent simulations of the sculling arm work-the movement from extension to flexion to extension.

The athlete commits to developing himself at a deeper level. With this quality and good coaching, any athlete can go a long way towards making up for deficiencies in natural talents. To facilitate this growth in the athlete the coach attempts to cultivate an open, creative, mind in each sculler. He encourages the athlete to abandon the security of conventional practices and thinking. He encourages the athlete to "explore" rather than to "exploit."

When Waldemar Cierpinski of East Germany, the 1976 Olympic Marathon winner, was asked about his coaches, he cited Jorg Ramlow. It was Ramlow who introduced him to the arts, discussions on literature, visits to the theater and listening to classical music. Ken Doherty, a long time track coach at the University of Pennsylvania, referred to this type of learning and teaching as holistic, where one's education, experience and practice are integrated.[10]

Twenty years ago Holger Geschwindner is credited with developing his protégé, Dirk Nowitzki, into the world's best non-American basketball player. This unconventional coach had been the captain of the German Olympic basketball team. He combined his knowledge of math and physics to develop Nowitzki's high arc shot curve. He also instructed Nowitzki to fence and row to increase his mobility and he encouraged Dirk to raise his "broadband literacy" by learning the saxophone and guitar.[11] In following this approach, Nowitzki expanded his consciousness indirectly assisted his improvement as a basketball player.

Both coaches were pushing their athletes expand their horizons and to explore new activities of the mind and body.

Fortunately, I had two coaches, Bob Fitzpatrick and Mike Yuhasz, who reinforced these thought patterns. Both men understood and promoted fluidity, one in sculling, and the other, wrestling. Both fully exploited the benefits of mastery training. For Fitzpatrick, you first had to master the release before progressing to the recovery. Yuhasz encouraged his athletes to learn a few basic moves, a ride, a takedown and a reverse. He emphasized simplicity. Certainly, their rational approaches to acquiring competency in technique captivated me. For maximum effect with this type of training, it is

---

[10] Harvey Araton, "Nowitski Moment Is a Footnote Back Home," *New York Times*, June 6, 2006 2006.

[11] Ken Wilber, *Integral Psychology: Consciousness, Spirit, Psychology, Therapy* (Boston, MA: Shambhala, 2000).

critical that the coach and athlete are totally committed to the process.

The Zen Monk, Shunryu Suzuki, offers a wise aphorism that is helpful: "In the beginner's mind there are many possibilities, in the expert's mind there are none."[12] By not relying on modeling, the athlete thinks and explores the unknown: thus his technique undergoes constant refinement. At the same time that the stroke-cycle is evolving, the sculler's awareness is also. Therefore, the "sweep" of the blades becomes an accurate metaphor for the scope and progress of the sculler's inner self, engaging the total spectrum of the mind, body and the spirit.

---

[12] Shunryu Suzuki and Trudy Dixon, *Zen Mind, Beginner's Mind*, 1st ed. (New York, NY: Weatherhill, 1970).

# Meditative Training

Systematic meditative practices, whether on water or land, develop a relaxed, quiet and focused mind, greatly assisting all aspects in the evolution of smooth movements. As meditation practice deepens, a stroke that is both subtle and effortless develops. The plasticity developed through meditation spills over into technique. Creative coaching shuffles the meditative practices into the technical and physical training.

Meditation is especially helpful practice in our unquiet, frenetic world of the 21st century. Slow unhurried movements are a basic feature of various Eastern Martial Arts practices. The rowing action performed in slow motion, both in and out of the shell allows the athlete to self-learn the sequence with higher levels of concentration and mindfulness. When the accuracy and rhythm reach perfection, the rowing motion is more fluid, providing a great foundation for race pace training. The athlete perfects the movements in slow motion so to be able to eventually move quickly.

Quiet sitting has both Eastern and Western origins; Parmenides, the Phoenician philosopher and father of logic, employed this practice as an effective healing process over 2,500 years ago. This practice of quiet sitting or lying still was a cornerstone to his teaching. For the modern athlete quiet sitting is an excellent device for stress reduction and focusing. Too often, we reject or dismiss the Eastern practices because of our lack of exposure to this ancient knowledge and because of our cultural imperialism.

Roger Bannister, in his wonderful little book, *The Four-Minute Mile*, underscores the importance of mental preparedness: "The mental approach is all important, because the strength and power of the mind are without limit. All this energy can be harnessed by the correct attitude of mind."[13] Banister, like Hanlan, was an excellent example of an athlete who observed himself, then recorded and analyzed his progress. This was simple science at work. I still value my sculling log from the 1950s, and as a coach I encourage athletes to maintain training logs. It is an excellent method for talking to oneself, recording setbacks, as well as progress

In today's distracting, fast-paced world, quiet meditation and time spent in the outdoors play a significant role in the athlete's development both as a person and performer. Including hiking, cross-country skiing, running and cycling, the athletes' cross training activities provide endless opportunities to experience the regenerative capacity of nature. Banister on the advice of his Swiss coach would climb mountains for a change from the training

---

[13] Roger Bannister, *The Four-Minute Mile* (New York: Lyons & Burford, 1989).

routine and to experience the recovery powers found in the solitude of climbing.

Finding solitude inside oneself, and stillness on the river are critical for the athlete's development. Much the way Hanlan experienced being alone on his lagoon. Somehow, today's athlete has to find similar quiet spaces and moments to advance his skill. We can also take a cue from the animals, observing that when they are injured they retreat to a quiet spot in the woods and sleep. We also need these quiet moments and spots to renew ourselves.

In a similar fashion, my quiet spot at Middletown, Connecticut was behind a fairly large island in the river. I tested the feel of using the blade as the fulcrum and comparing it to the feel of using the pin as the fulcrum of the lever. After a certain amount of experimenting, I returned to the standard practice of using the pin for my levering. To this day, on many occasions I return to my favorite place on the river to rejuvenate my coaching.

Observation of self and how you move is the starting point. You attempt to have your feet flow with the earth's surface rather than having a jarring intersection of the two components. It is almost a gliding motion that conserves energy and produces fluidity. Walking is the one activity that one can form the basis of practice for flow. Henry David Thoreau had the same experience in the woods around Walden Pond. I have always encouraged the college athletes to park their vehicles and walk the beautiful campus.

Still water is extremely helpful for this process of observation, analyzing, experimenting and modifying. For me, St. Catharines was an ideal setting for this. The training was amplified because my coach remained on the bank insuring quiet space for my introspection. The two factors of smooth water and absentee coach were extremely important for achieving competency with a totally different technique and strategy for the quarter mile race.

    The technique called for a finish of the body at the perpendicular with the hands in front of the abdominal wall. At the other end of the slide the reach was shortened to just past the toes. The strategy had a standard 20 stroke start followed by 10 strokes at 32 taking advantage of momentum from the high stroke start, followed by a quick build up of the rate with the same stroke length to the finish line. The strategy provided a rest and regeneration phase of 10 strokes. With this approach, I was always competitive in the short race. This unique strategy was an excellent example of creative coaching and athletic efficiency.

    Hanlan is an excellent metaphor for Flow and a modern stroke. His modifications of the drive phase are testimony to this assessment. Lengthening the track gave him additional reach, and emphasized his leg power. With the longer track he was able to move his legs closer to the midline. The correction eliminated his previously over splayed legs creating a more linear and powerful involvement of this important dimension of his stroke. With this change the trunk was less between the legs, but rather armpits over the knees. Posture was more upright. His influence is observed in photos of scullers that followed him, especially the Canadians, such as Jake Gaudaur and Lou Scholes, and the American Ten Eycks. From old photos one can see the advanced muscle definition of his arms is also mirrored in his legs. Hanlan was the complete athlete, extremely fit, mentally astute, and probably one of the finest technical scullers in the history of the sport.

One of the primary benefits of practicing for smooth movement is the development of concentration, "the merging of action and awareness that is made possible by the centering on a limited stimulus field."[14] To insure that people will concentrate on their actions, the effects of the intruding stimuli must be minimized; this involves a narrowing of consciousness and returning to concentrating on the breathing.

Geoffrey Page, a British rowing coach, wrote the following in 1963: "Rowing is a sport requiring intense and sustained concentration. Unless a crew can be trained to keep its mind on the job the clearance will diminish and the blade work will get "woolly" towards the end of any stretch of work. The crew must learn to think independently and to judge the pace of the boat; the crew must not rely on the coach to do it for them."[15]

The athletes taking the initiative by being more concentrated in their training and racing are acting as "first hand" athletes. The first hand athlete is operating for long periods on his own. The coach cannot always be present especially in a sport like rowing with its lakes and rivers as practice venues. Rowing is not confined to relatively small areas like other sports that train and compete in the tight space of a gym or arena.

---

[14] Mihaly Csikszentmihalyi, "Play and Intrinsic Rewards," *Journal of Humanistic Psychology* 15, no. 3 (1975).

[15] Geoffrey Page, *Coaching for Rowing* (London,: Museum Press, 1963), 36.

Concentration is balanced with mindfulness, which is our ability to stay in the present moment. Thus we must learn to remain focused in the present moment: "knowing what you are doing, while you are doing it, no matter what it may be."[16] This quality must be reinforced on the water, in the weight room, on the ergometer and during any cross training activity. Parmenides referred to this quality as the Reality of the Now. Past or future do not enter into our thinking as we are fully centered in the present.

Creating a systematic plan for mental training insures that it is integrated into the overall race preparation and into the daily life of the athlete. The mental training begins with the first fall practice session and is a daily occurrence thereafter in some form or another. The athlete should meditate for a minimum of 10 to 15 minutes during each practice session both on and off the water.[17] To summarize, the athlete begins by sitting quietly, slowing down, observing and feeling, becoming fully attentive and aware, and finally by learning to remain in the present moment - mindfulness. This type of regular training creates a pronounced change.

The practice of mindfulness can eventually lead to a state where the self is minimized, and we become

---

[16] Jimmy Joy, *The Mind's Eye: Mental Training for the Coach* (New York: Joy of Sculling, 2002).

[17] For the William Smith College Women's crew from 1994 to 1999, the mental training plan was an integral part of the training. The women developed into dedicated and accomplished meditators and were recognized for their consistency, and spirited racing.

immersed in "bare awareness."[18] This is our essential awareness that is buried under layers of thought and identity, including reaction and adaptation. Bare awareness for the athlete is both physical and mental. The athlete strips the body of unnecessary muscular action, and the mind becomes free of any baggage. This is really a process of simplifying our sculling and our life by economizing.

Modern leaders such as Fridjof Nansen, Ernest Shackleton, and T.E. Lawrence adopted this mindset because of the challenges of their respective environments: Nansen in the Arctic, Shackleton in Antarctica, and Lawrence in Arabia. They were forced to minimize the energy spent by the body and mind as they met the rigors of their respective environments. The athlete who undergoes rigorous daily training experiences somewhat similar challenges but then has respite from the regimen during the recovery part of the day. My three exemplars of leadership did not have this break from their daily hardships. They faced the challenges continuously. It was a life or death struggle for them and their followers and enhanced their lives.

It takes long and continuous practice of mindful meditation to gain an initial glimpse of the potential of this highly evolved state. With this finely tuned and sensitive awareness, the body becomes extremely resilient. Old coaches referred to it as "the point of the needle." This was the situation facing Nansen, Lawrence and Shackleton. Similarly, the gifted well-trained athlete reaches this level of fine

---

[18] Daniel J. Siegel, *The Mindful Brain : Reflection and Attunement in the Cultivation of Well-Being*, 1st ed. (New York: W.W. Norton, 2007).

body tuning and awareness. Thus it is important to be aware of the potential of systematic training and the possible changes that can occur with constant and consistent training during our athletic years and beyond.

Our emotional state in training, racing and life beyond the shell must not be overlooked. An awareness, accessibility and release of emotion is essential to good sculling. Failure to do so may result in less than optimal performance outcomes.

The highly trained athlete explores his mind with a focused attention that Dr. Daniel Siegel calls Mindsight. This is the body's wisdom accessed through interoception or "perceiving within." An excellent quality to practice is our ability to be conscious of our awareness by going inside of ourselves. My coach encouraged his scullers to take a moment to self-reflect before each training piece. Thus we learned to act from our inner being. Two obvious indicators for perceiving the "elusive" within are the breath and heart rates. Another example is applying the same conscientious internal monitoring to each stroke. This was done with 20 stroke high pieces where each stroke in the 30 seconds was evaluated.

Our enhanced inner self and flexibility in the brain serve as a balance to modern man's mechanistic analytical patterns of thought and movement. Recent research demonstrates that there is more opportunity for neuronal development if there is variety in the training program as found in physiological adaptation. Plasticity is recognized as occurring in the brain as well as the body.

The mind's natural state of integration includes body, mind, emotions, and spirit. Our awareness of integration comes from observing our immediate environment and beyond our own skin. Once this is understood it is immediately applicable to technique and flow.

In this high level state of mindfulness, awareness extends beyond the boundaries of the body and engages in a non-dualistic world. So the gifted athlete may sometime experience moments of bare awareness in his sport. The athlete begins to be aware that he is not a separate self from the coach, teammates or natural world beyond the confines of his body and his mind. He connects with the shell, wind, waves and water to become an intimate segment of this larger world. For Hanlan this connection came from vagaries of his Toronto Harbor home and his international racing. The interdependency of these components combined to create a unique qualitative component as well as a quantitative aspect to his sculling and his life.

The coach tries to stimulate the hunger in the mind of the young athlete for knowledge - technical, intellectual, physical, emotional, and spiritual - a lifelong journey. The thirst for variety, novelty and neuronal change has never left me. It has grown even stronger over time.

Are we as coaches digging deep enough into our own sporting past? This is what makes Hanlan so important and full of lessons for the modern sculler.

Usually a person who ends up coaching after his competitive days realizes that, "if he only knew then what he knows now, how much better an athlete he would have been." The coach can accelerate the athlete's knowledge by three simple methods: distributing mental training literature on a regular basis; the coach's daily pre-practice technical demonstrations; and regular meditation practice. The technical demonstration is particularly helpful for the athlete because it is a time that he can ask specific questions. It is also important for the coach because he maintains his technical connection to the sport. So, it is a situation where the bond and communication between the coach and the athletes is strengthened.

Many hours of visualization, quiet sitting, relaxation and concentration periods integrated into the program trains the mind. These practices are easy to incorporate into the training program and they add intensity to the training needed for growth and adaptation. The benefits of the meditation within the integrated coaching approach are immense to the education of the athlete. The athlete learns to focus and concentrate, become more aware, calmer and controlled, as development of the invaluable skill of visualization continues to develop.

My initial encounter with the important practice of visualization occurred over 50 years ago when my sculling coach encouraged me to see the stroke cycle with the "Mind's Eye." "And it is only when one can feel and taste the 'sweetness' of the harmony of movement of the body and the run of the shell, that a sculling image can be seen in the mind's eye of Fitzpatrick."[19]

In our rowing culture, the dominance of quantity is reflected in the prominence of the ergometer score; yet, there are other uses for this machine besides testing, including training, drills and highly effective simulation exercises. The

---

[19] Jimmy Joy, "The Art of Sculling," in *NAAO (Now USRA) Annual Meeting* (Syracuse, NY1978).

simulation exercises performed without the oar break the stroke into parts and then multiple repetitions are executed on each of the parts. Fitzpatrick's use of the simulation exercises was a stroke of genius as the exercises are a "pump-primer" for visualization. These drills really help to make the coach and the athlete aware of the whole stroke. The simulation exercises also have the effect of slowing down the athletes' movements to perfect the skills. It is a simple exercise of pruning the unnecessary from the stroke cycle. Accuracy becomes the priority over power for the moment.

Variations of the simulation exercises develop the precision in the individual and group timing and they evolve into mindfulness training of slow motion rowing. The drills ingrain the precision of group timing. Place the machines side-by-side as the coach guides the athletes 'up and down' the slide bed calling out where to stop at the various slide segments – o, ¼, ½, ¾, full. The coach then checks the accuracy of the seat positions, leg and trunk angles. Eventually the athletes reach absolute uniformity at the various positions. The scheduling of these simulation exercises in the training program requires creativity from the coach. However, these drills are essential for establishing timing, uniformity and economy in the stroke cycle.

Meditative stability refers to the ability to extend the attention level from a few minutes to 10 to 30 minutes with regular training. To begin the practice session, sit with good posture and take a few deep breaths to settle your mind, then focus on breathing normally. After a few deep inhalations, concentrate on your breathing allowing the air to effortlessly flow in and out. Instead of observing your breathing, you can begin to count the number of inhales and exhales. If the mind starts to wander, make note of it and bring it back to focus. Gradually increase your sitting time. Devise a yearly training cycle that accommodates both the total environment and academic schedule of the athlete.

# Training the Spirit - Mindfulness

The initial step for developing Mindfulness is to slow down the pace of life, unplug from technology and experience the power generated from sitting, walking or rowing silently. This develops our inner self or spirit and in effect becomes our essential being. Mindfulness training expands our window of tolerance, allowing us to become more resilient, less judgmental less distracted by outside events and situations and more accepting of self and others.[20] We tend to concentrate on our inner self and become less attracted to the materialistic world.

One form of mind activity is narrowly focused like the lens of a microscope and the other has a broad focus similar to a macro lens. Effective movement is the ability to differentiate between the lens' telescoping ability by zooming in for a close-up, or out for a more sweeping perspective. An example of "zooming in" is watching the hands for levelness at the entry and feeling the knuckles nudging the abdominal wall at the release. For an expanded

---

[20] Siegel, *The Mindful Brain : Reflection and Attunement in the Cultivation of Well-Being.*

consciousness, effective mindfulness is observing the action of the stern at the blade entry.

The Spirit has two levels, the intrinsic and the elevated. On the first, spirit permeates the training and our daily life (immanence). For this to occur, both consistency and intensity are required. However, this spirit is our inner strength, fostering the effective functioning of the whole organism. This requires a strong attentiveness. The mind remains in the present rather than on past failure or future success, or visions of glory. By centering in the present "you know what you are doing, while you are doing it, no matter what it may be." This quality surfaces in the athlete's consistency of performance.

On the second level, it is also the expression of the highest level of athletic expression (transcendence). This is the evolution of the self to a higher level of being and doing. Ken Wilber employs the ladder analogy where the spirit is the wood of the ladder (immanence) and the highest rung of the ladder (transcendence). Therefore the athlete, while simultaneously present in the moment, is engaged in embracing the rungs just beyond his reach, while continuing the climb. Wilber states, "The clear, simple, spontaneous, effortless awareness of whatever is happening in this moment is the ever-present Spirit, or Mindfulness." Georg Feurstein's definition of spirit is helpful and contains both qualities in a simple sentence: "spirit means any value, thought, attitude, impulse, mood, disposition, bodily behavior or action when going beyond the individual self."[21]

**Diagram 3 - The Flow Staircase**

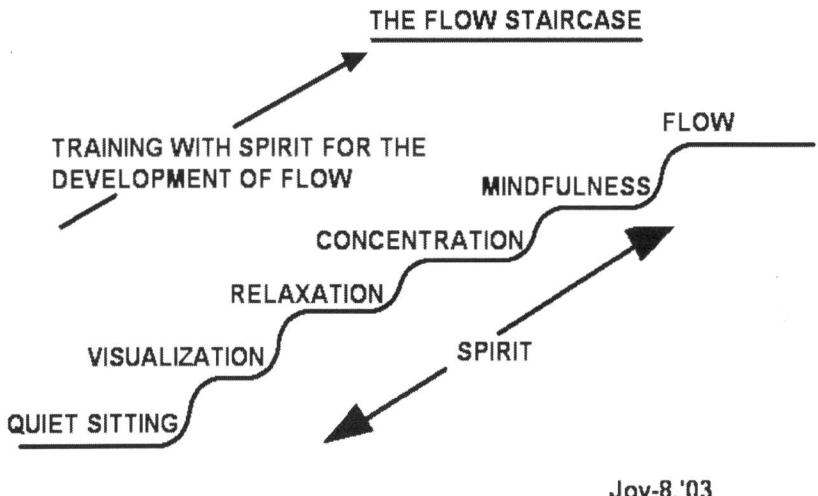

With constant practice concentration, relaxation and mindfulness evolve into higher states of awareness (see Diagram 3). Similarly, these are the characteristics of outstanding performers like Jim Brown, Michael Jordan, Rory McIlroy and Wayne Gretzky. These athletes were very aware of all action within the playing area. Gretzky, in particular, knew at every moment where his opponents, the puck, the goal and his teammates were located. He always operated with a high degree of mindfulness. Remember that Gretzky was precocious and successful in his early teens. The combination of concentration, relaxation and mindfulness are the highly valued ingredients of economy and conservation of energy.

---

[21] Georg Feuerstein, *Structures of Consciousness: The Genius of Jean Gebser - an Introduction and Critique* (Lower Lake, CA: Integral Publishing, 1987).

I will always recall being mindful doing three 20-stroke high rate pieces for quickness and precision at the end of most workouts. The coach wanted me to monitor each of the strokes over the half minute. I remember how in the early part of the season the release movements were rough and hurried. However, later they would become rhythmic and fluid. The wrists would evolve from a pronounced downward break to a much more subtle flowing action. I came to realize intuitively the good and bad strokes. It was immediate. This exercise in quickness, precision, mindfulness and intuitive non-thinking would remain in my memory bank for the rest of my life. The way the coach inserted mindfulness and technique into a high-pressure physical exercise was wonderful training.

The athlete's personal development is optimized when there is a "oneness" between the environment and the whole person, and between our internal and external selves. The performance becomes fully integrative combining the body, emotions, mind and spirit. This is evident when the athlete is able to coordinate his body action, and then integrate these movements with the run of the shell. This is Flow. In a 1978 paper, *The Art of Sculling*, I wrote: "the sculler is a skilled athlete and artist constantly reaching for more sublime levels of skill and performance. His or her sculling is an art form-beautiful (like Ruth's swing), graceful, powerful, rhythmic, and speedy."[22]

At this point the training objective makes a significant shift, moving from skill training to placing more emphasis on the athlete's self development. As Herrigel writes in *Zen in the Art of Archery*, "the origin

---

[22] Joy, "The Art of Sculling."

of ability in the athlete is to be sought in spiritual exercises, and the aim of the athlete consists in hitting a spiritual goal, so that fundamentally the marksman aims at himself and may even succeed in hitting himself."[23]

The individual's spirit is fostered by the coach with the team working as a unit and by empowering the athletes in their training. The athlete is encouraged to create and discover new ways of refining the movements. The coach trusts the athlete to explore, to fail and to achieve.

This development of spirit contributes to the athlete's inner strength and his ability to be more functionally effective as he uses his whole body. The martial arts master Shi Ming feels that this consciousness "is a kind of developed mind in which the biological and the psychological are forged together as one." Further, he defines this consciousness, "as a comprehensive structure uniting philosophy, psychology, medical science, principles and techniques of self defense, dynamics, energetics, quintessential ethics, fine arts, and numerous other fields of science and culture."[24]

There is much that can be learned from these 1,000-2,000 year old practices of yoga, tai chi, aikido and other martial arts on how to generate power effectively and effortlessly. The easy way to make use of these practices on water is to do slow motion rowing. Slow motion rowing is used in a number of ways, including as part of the warm up, in between

---

[23] Eugen Herrigel, *Zen in the Art of Archery* (New York, NY: Vintage Books, 1989).

[24] Shi Ming, *Mind over Matter: Higher Martial Arts* (Berkeley, CA: North Atlantic Books, 1994).

rd pieces, to aid recovery, to separate steady state rills and as cool down trying to achieve the least number of strokes per minute. With this type of practice the athlete can see and feel the accuracy and rhythm of the stroke cycle. The athlete develops a deeper understanding of the various movements while he is doing the skill. Consequently, the stroke cycle begins to permeate his whole being with the spirit being the bridge between the body and the mind (see Diagram 3).

Dr. Roger Bannister, after he broke the four-minute mile barrier, concluded in his book, "the human spirit is indomitable."[25]

---

[25] Bannister, *The Four-Minute Mile*.

# Silence, Stillness, Simplicity

*Except for the point, the stillpoint,*

*There would be no dance,*

*And there is only dance.*
                          T.S. Eliot

These three integrated and powerful qualities go a long way to producing economy of motion. From the power of stillness and silence in the body and mind, the movements become more efficient (economical and instinctive), "awareness and action merge," and the smooth actions become even more subtle and reproducible. Given the distractions that we face in our everyday existence finding stillness in body and mind might be extremely difficult qualities to cultivate. Spending time in the woods, park or green spaces of a college campus during early morning training are helpful ways to experience stillness and quiet.

Instincts and feeling are developed by slow motion rowing, quiet non-coached long rows, cross training in "nature," and the constant reinforcement of mindfulness in training. The cross training is inly to develop the athlete's athleticism and his nnection with the environment. At this point our culling becomes smoother and more instinctual.

Simplicity is the key for achieving efficiency. It is part of our deep bond with the environment and our immediate landscape is our body. Simplifying is also a form of body sculpturing where the unnecessary movements are eliminated. Only the essential motions and muscle actions remain producing a smooth skill pattern. The athlete has to feel the conservation in his movements. This is a deeper sense of being that fosters a host of feelings such as awareness, patience, control, accuracy and confidence. In observing the skilled athlete, these qualities are apparent. An excellent way to feel this conservation is mindful training on the ergometer, consciously observing the subtle shifts between activity and stillness in the specific muscle groups. The stillness can be directly related to the degree of energy conservation achieved. This is one of the primary elements in the training.

Christy Mathewson,[26] the Hall of Fame baseball pitcher, was effective for so long because he was efficient guided by the knowledge of just how much energy was needed in a given situation. Mathewson, facing a difficult hitter such as Honus Wagner, attempted to have him pop-up on the first pitch, rather than waste his energy on the fastballs that might or might not result in a strikeout. This is the same quality of economy that characterized Hanlan's sculling throughout the various parts of his stroke.

---

[26] Christy Mathewson won 373 games in his major league baseball career

Perfecting the individual movements comes through patient practice. You never rush the process of skill acquisition. Each fragment has a logical and economical foundation. These fundamentals lead the athlete to have simplicity as a goal with his training in the shell, and his life.

The effective coach is patient with the progress of the sculler's technique, instilling confidence in the athlete, as he moves to higher and more sublime levels of perfection. He must find the power of the stillness in his coaching. Sitting with his athletes during their meditation sessions is very helpful.

If the adage "busy minds make for busy bodies," then moments of stillness are critical. The process of training for flow begins with periods of quiet sitting designed to enhance the experience. It is important that the coach and athlete develop these qualities, as this type of practice will form the foundation for mindfulness.

All meditative practices are employed either as separate training components or woven into other aspects of athletic conditioning. The creation of increased focus, concentration, and development of intuition gained from these activities accelerate the learning process. The result is instinct. For example, the recovery phase for example, eventually develops into an unthinking instinct to simply glide forward.

Is it possible to retrieve this particularly beautiful and sensitive dimension in our sport from a mechanistic world? To do so the successful athlete must be challenged physically and mentally, largely without the benefit of technology, to access this primordial state of being. Sculling provides the perfect opportunity to develop this aspect of deeper

…nctual nature by intricately connecting the …ller to nature, much the way animals and birds …nd effortlessly with the environment.

The instinct to move quickly without thinking is critical when racing. Watching the flight of the birds we see the stroke of the bird's wings perform a series of intricate movements merged into a smooth fluid unitary motion. Similarly, the athlete and the shell display the same integration while moving effortlessly, creating a highly evolved state of intuitive action, allowing the shell to slide elegantly through the water.

Yes, we might have to adjust the technique to the conditions but there is no thinking involved. It is an immediate reaction to what we feel through our relaxed hands. For example, the hands react quickly to the rough conditions and become absorbers of the wave action.

The early stages of training emphasize large movements in the cycle such as the leg drive, trunk swing, and arm draw, and provide opportunities for the athletes to experience a rough feel for the movement. Later, the focus shifts to the specific parts with the athletes striving to perform subtle and economical movements. As stated earlier, the simulation exercises are a good place to use this coaching approach. In any given year during the final stages of practice use whole movements where the objective is to integrate the body action with the oar and shell run. It is a process of ingraining the pattern into the body wisdom.

The psychologist Mihaly Cziksentmihaly summarizes this idea concisely: "flow denotes the holistic sensation present when we act with a total involvement. It is a state in which action follows upon action according to an internal logic which seems to need no conscious intervention on our part."[27] This "internal logic" or intuition recalls a story told to me by my own coach, Bob Fitzpatrick.[28] "During a practice Coach Fitzpatrick reached for the megaphone to make a comment to the sculler. He observed Bob's movement and immediately made the targeted technical adjustment without a word spoken. According to the impeccable Fitzpatrick, this amazing communication occurred on two more occasions during the practice, a beautiful example of intelligent sculling and coaching."[29] This is an excellent example of the intuitional state that develops between coach and athlete.

Finally, Stephen Mitchell explains this state of mind and body clearly: "A good athlete can enter a state of body awareness in which the right stroke or the right movement happens by itself, effortlessly,

---

[27] Csikszentmihalyi, "Play and Intrinsic Rewards."

[28] Fitzpatrick's coaching, founded in his technique roots that included training from an Olympic coach, John O'Neill, who was the coach of Olympic Champion, Frank Greer at the turn of the 19thCentury. Fitzpatrick also followed the sculling methods of the Ten Eycks from Syracuse. This background gave Fitzpatrick a thorough grounding in the English Orthodox technique. This technique would undergo some significant modification in the 1930s with his coaching of Bob Pearce, the Olympic Champion and with his exposure to Fairbairn's methods at the 1932 Olympics in Los Angeles. Fitzpatrick in his own way remained a Traditionalist by taking the best parts from each of these methods and molding the methods into a single effective technique. Thus, over 70 years ago, this little known Canadian coach from Nova Scotia had come up with an efficient synthesis from four very successful sources – Orthodoxy, Fairbairn, Ten Eyck, and Pearce. He resisted the temptation to model the latest technical trend. His stroke was rational, energy efficient and is still very effective today.

[29] Joy, "The Art of Sculling."

without any interference of the conscious will."[30] Sculling and rowing in such an intuitive state captures the whole of Hanlan's spirit.

Intuition is our ability to understand something immediately, without the need for conscious reasoning. This type of subtle knowledge by the mind and body allows the athlete to Flow. A helpful step for developing intuition is to slow down the pace of life. Then we are able to observe, analyze and further our understanding of ourselves in the external world.

Both quiet sitting and slow motion rowing develop these qualities. Slow motion rowing is a form of active quiet sitting. Phil Jackson, former coach of the Los Angeles Lakers, had silent practices of 90 minutes' duration. A rowing practice can be very effective if done periodically in total silence. The silence is interrupted only by the occasional commands of the coxswain.

At the more advanced levels of sculling, a very high degree of monitoring and biofeedback occurs. The coach merely affirms the skill of the performing artist. The coach is rather an odd combination of parent, leader and choreographer.[31]

The rowing coach and his athletes are not separate selves encapsulated in their skin, but are a resilient part of the unpredictable environment of wind, water and waves. They are intensely involved through the beauty of the fall, the rigors of early winter and spring, to the hot summers. The great

---

[30] Stephen Mitchell, *Tao Te Ching* (New York, NY: Harper, 1988).

[31] Joy, "The Art of Sculling."

Czech runner Emil Zatopek[32] remarked, "If it is raining, what does it matter? If it is snowing, what does it matter?" This reminds me of my winter coaching on the beautiful campus of Hobart and William Smith Colleges. The undulating terrain of the campus and a nice long hill in the middle of the grounds were perfect settings for wintery runs and long bouts of hill training. The athletes were reminded that they were vikings. I guess I could have referred to them as Zatopeks. They were toughened with this type of regimen using the bounty of the winter blasts.

Effective rowing coaches possess the same nature-based philosophy. Wendell Berry the wonderful 20th Century agrarian writer advocates a simple, nature-based style of living that parallels the type of Mennonite existence that we are witness to in the Finger Lakes region of Western New York State. It doesn't mean that we all have to be farmers or return to the land but we can adopt the philosophy of economy, simplicity, and conservation of energy by being in touch with ourselves, our bodies and our immediate environment. As such, the rowing coach is an amphibian moving between the world of his boathouse, the weight and erg room, and the vicissitudes of the river.

Hanlan's Point on Toronto Island has an air of tranquility and timelessness to it. One can project and imagine the setting for the young Hanlan in the late 19th Century. It was a perfect haven for his moments of reflection on the stroke cycle and life and for his technique work. You need to make it habit to

---

[32] Emil Zatopek won the 5,000m, 10,000m, and Marathon at the 1952 Olympic Games.

reflect before your pieces in training. What do you hope to accomplish with this particular 500 or 1,000 meters? Can you see the stroke pattern that you hope to produce in this next piece? This practice should be an important part of your training method. The old coach insisted on this practice with his scullers.

    With this type of comprehensive mental training, the athlete's internal core develops strength, stability, and quiet confidence. With these valuable qualities, the sculling stroke becomes part of your being; it becomes your posture, flexibility, accuracy, relaxation, timing, agility, concentration and rhythm all synchronized into one powerful movement. In the athlete's mind, athleticism and the simple objective of smooth movements must be foremost in executing the training program.

# Essential Elements

The essential physical elements for developing the smoothness of movement and flow are posture, relaxation, flexibility, timing, economy, accuracy and rhythm (see Diagram 2, The Bridge). Two excellent exercises for flexibility and rhythm are yoga and the rope jump. Yoga enhances the range of motion and, ultimately, the athlete's potential power. The rope jump stimulates our innate body rhythms and sense of timing. Both forms of training develop athleticism. Pushing the shell from the dock by all eight and occasionally standing up in the shell are two additional exercises to develop the crew's athleticism. These skills require good balance, agility, and coordination. We use our natural body rhythms to learn to dance and sculling is a seated dance. With any improvement in skill energy is conserved.

In the early stages of training posture and relaxation are emphasized along with the regular practice of quiet sitting, yoga and drills that develop the athletes' concentration levels. The posture of the trunk is monitored in and out of the shell, in running, lifting weights, on the ergometer, during yoga or any other activity. This monitoring is the responsibility of both coach and athlete. Importantly, posture also includes the natural alignment of the head, trunk, hips and legs both on land and in the shell. Again constant monitoring by the coach is critical. The proper posture of trunk will insure that the body is relaxed.

Relaxation is an essential factor for an effective drive in rowing; a relaxed motion during the drive phase allows for full utilization of the athlete's power potential. During this phase the arms move easily from extension to flexion, the legs push down with a steady even pressure, and the trunk action with its subtle arc over the full length of the slide keeps the shoulders level.

The relaxed powerful drive results from the light hands, fluid elbow action and the steady legwork. In the *Art of Sculling*, I write, "The mind and muscle (proprioception) are trained to be sensitive to the individual movements and the movement of the body in the shell." This awareness is centered largely in the hands as they monitor the neat, accurate entry of the blade and fluid pressure throughout the drive. Other specific locations in the body, namely the shoulders and legs, also feel the effect of efficient productive blade work.

Relaxation is developed by a number of methods including: by partner assisted lowering of the shoulders called shoulder resets, by training at 90% effort during intensity sessions, by slow motion rowing, by easy speeds workouts where the rate of stroking is raised from 30 to 40 over 30 strokes and by alternating relaxed strokes with high tension ones. Actually, you cannot have economy without relaxation and, "through relaxing we not only have a supple body, but we've calmed our mind in the process"[33]

The initial instruction for both posture and relaxation is the hand placement on the oar handles. The handles are held lightly, so that there is "play" between the hands and the instrument, just as sculling in the larger sense is childlike play.

A good example of this is how the skilled Bob Pearce used his fingers to square and feather the blade with the wrists remaining flat. Initially, the hands are positioned with flat wrists when the blade is squared in the water. The handles are held between the pads, the roots of the fingers (where the fingers meet the hand) and the fingers with the knuckle line on top of the handle. When you release the blade the handle moves to a position resting between the roots of the fingers and the actual fingers. At the release the knuckle line is parallel to the long axis of the handle. However, at the entry the hand position shifts so that the knuckle line is at an angle to the long axis of the handle. The thumb is always on the end of the handle exerting lateral pressure. The innermost finger is positioned at the edge of the handle. With this position of the hands and fingers there is no strain on the hands, fingers or wrists. The ability to engage only the required muscle groups enhances the athlete's ability to relax and conserve energy. This is an example of active stillness and simplicity.

---

[33] Peter Ralston, *Cheng Hsin : The Principles of Effortless Power*, 2nd ed. (Berkeley, Calif.: North Atlantic Books, 1999).

**Diagram 4 - The relaxed hand, from Richard Burnell's <u>The Oxford Pocketbook of Sculling Training</u>**

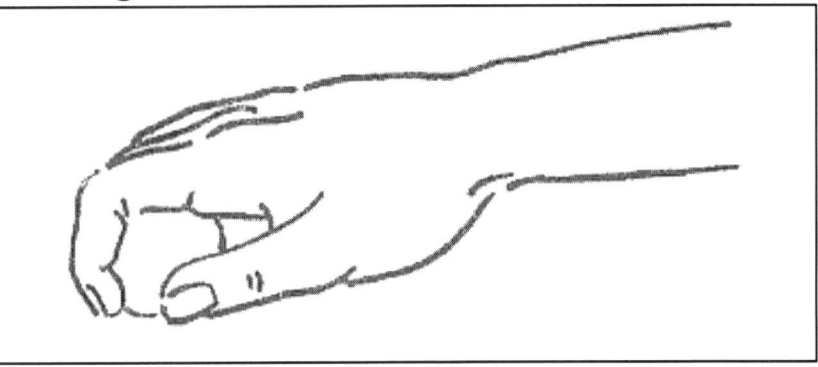

From old photographs of Hanlan, his erect yet relaxed posture, and totally extended body are evident. The viewer is looking at a classic sculler, similar to someone looking at Babe Ruth swinging a bat in 1927. Another striking example from the 1950s and the 1960s was the running style of football's Jim Brown. His powerful upper body was still and poised. The same potential for fluidity is present no matter what historical sporting era is investigated.

The careful developmental progression of these elements and the unhurried action of the various movements improve the athleticism of the individual leading to simplicity of the whole stroke motion. A bridge is created between the basic technical and physical training and the development of fluid motion by emphasizing each of these elements in the training. Ken Wilber reminds us that, "one must master the body's subtle energies and movements to master the mind."[34] The coach is like a sculptor at this point. He is gradually and patiently chiseling off the rough edges of the technique in the athlete. The critical question is, do you want to be an artful Sculler or a brute force Slugger? The sculler has to be aware that the sensitivity of the single is less forgiving of extraneous movements than the larger eight. This requires constant and patient practice for refinement of the stroke.

Emphasizing smooth movements and wholeness rather than fragmentation becomes the central focus for the training. It is the umbrella quality for each of the training components including the physiological, psychological, and technical. You can feel this unique focus becoming a part of your unified life. Today's physicists recognize the importance of wholeness evolving towards greater integration and oneness. For rowing, this is exemplified in the stroke cycle of the accomplished sculler. As part of this evolution your awareness sharpens and becomes more expansive. Awareness is the 'trimming knife' employed to reshape the neural pathways because with the heightened attention, neuroplasticity is enhanced. With this increased plasticity you become more open, flexible and adaptable. The old East German literature referred to this concept of plasticity as "dynamic stereotypes" and the Germans felt that it was achieved through variety in the training and by emphasizing sculling for young athletes.

I remember, as a boy, observing the easy motion of workers cutting the long grass bordering

---

[34] Wilber, *Integral Psychology: Consciousness, Spirit, Psychology, Therapy.*

the Canadian National Railway line in St. Catharines, Ontario. Consequently, the rhythmic movement of the workers' arms extending and flexing was mesmerizing. There was a grace, rhythm, and power to their effortless movements. These were working athletes with an established stroke pattern that could be easily altered slightly depending on the configuration of the grassy terrain. It approximated the sculling stroke with its consistent limits at each end of the slide but with its equivalent ability to adjust to water and wind conditions.

 I was also fortunate to have a father who was an outstanding multi-sport athlete in his youth before the Great War of 1914 wreaked havoc on his body leaving him with numerous wounds and a partially amputated foot. However, you could still see remnants of what were the strong, flowing movements of his youth. He flowed as he simulated his powerful and quick boxing moves. His soccer footwork was still there even at an advanced age. The golf and badminton swings were still fluid despite the partial foot. Occasionally, for a short burst he would display his track speed and prowess. The last time that he used this skill was in 1917 where he was a runner during the famous Battle of Vimy Ridge. I also admired his photography skills and how he managed his equipment across the locks on the Welland Ship Canal. Even at an advanced age he was still the fearless, agile athlete in his role of government photographer.

 This practice of observation has remained with me throughout the years. These examples, like my father, were for me quite close at hand. You have to be aware of the ordinary situations in everyday life that have some application to your sculling and overall awareness of fluid motion. So, in addition to watching these skilled, fluid workers, my attention was drawn to the movements of the neighborhood cats and dogs, admiring their athleticism.

In the sculling stroke, at one end, the knees are in the armpits for executing the entry and at the opposite end of the slide the trunk and legs finish together supporting the release of the blade. However, within the confines of the stroke there is ample room for improvement and refinement of the movements. The consistency in stroke length produces a rhythmic pattern much like Hanlan's. He could maintain a rating of 34 to 36 strokes per minute over long distances. An aggressive stroke action is created through the stroke's disciplined tightness, and the absence of loose ends. This is the moment when the shell and body come together to create flow.

Timing, rhythm and refinement take time to develop and are enhanced with repetition and duration. Refinement refers to increasing the subtleness of physical action and this quality has a direct relationship to economy of motion. The movements must be economical, without any extraneous motion. I recall watching the British entry, Paula Radcliffe, in the 2008 Olympic Games Women's Marathon, and observing how much extra movement there was to her head. It was evident to the viewer that the she would not finish the race. There was too much impedimenta in her running technique, the unnecessary baggage. The winner of the event had a more economical stride.

Timing is developed effectively through the simulation exercises during the winter preparation period and is so effective in developing a balanced platform at the gunwales. With three to four weeks of simulation exercises the balance is near perfect when the crews experience their first spring day on the water. Visiting Yaz Farooq, I saw a picture of her 1995 World Championship Crew and pointed out the discrepancies in the leg angles during the drive, so the timing was far from perfected.

    Drilling extensively with concentrated intensity using simulation exercises can correct these discrepancies. Place the machines side by side and have the athletes work without the handles moving to various positions on the slide at the coach's command. The coach corrects the angles of trunk and legs. These are low technology but highly effective practices.

# The Rough Phase - Three Major Body Movements

Timing, economy, refinement, and rhythm have to be developed in the three major body movements of the trunk, legs, hands and arms. When teaching the three major body movements of the legs, arms and trunk to novices on the ergometer, minimize the instruction. Too much verbiage by the coach at this stage simply creates chaos in the brain of the young athlete. The objective for each of these movements is a smooth transition from flexion to extension.

Teaching the three basic motions is where the coach should start in working to make a crew's actions uniform. The issue of movement homogeneity should be addressed by college and national team coaches who find themselves dealing with different techniques. The arm draw has to be a fluid transition and not a severe yank or tug of the handle. The legs move down and up with a steady firm motion rather than an explosive thrust. The trunk swing is subtle and horizontal on the drive and well timed with the seat on the recovery. When the three movements have a fair degree of mastery then the release and entry are addressed. Technique training is an evolution from the rough stage each fall to the more refined stage of summer. Patience, and openness to change, are required by both the coach and athlete.

    The body is integrated with the blade work that includes smooth transitions of the blade action at each end of the stroke — "lower edge and flat wrist rowing' — and the even pressure on the blades during the drive (pulling what you can handle). The blade actions can be simulated effectively using the hands. The total stroke integration can be practiced on land using the trunk simulations, as well as from a sitting position focusing on the movements of the body swing, leg drive and blade work. It is an excellent tool for learning the stroke cycle out of the shell. The simulations can be done in a number of ways. The first includes the use of the hands to describe the entry and release; another using a leg up on a bench to simulate the trunk and leg action, as well as for group timing; another sitting a group on a bench for the timing of the trunk swing, using the ergometer without the handle and breaking the stroke cycle into parts and doing multiple repeats.

    It is important to try to visualize the connection to the blade action as the simulations are practiced. This type of drilling establishes the rowing motion as a well-timed continuum with a subtle trunk swing, from stroke to stroke (see *The Mind's Eye* by this author). Simulation exercises practiced out of the shell assist immensely in developing the coordination between the legs, trunk, hands and arms. Also, the exercises help to establish the blade and body movements as an essential part of your deeper being. You are the stroke, the smooth stroke. During the early stages of practice, the athletes slow the movements so that they can feel and monitor the accuracy of the whole body engaged in the stroke cycle, especially during the "striding" of the body during the drive phase. Slow motion to complete the practice is also effective way to end the outing. This is the Tai Chi of sculling. By moving slowly the athlete can analyze the accuracy of his movements.

# The Smooth Phase - Refinement of the Fragments

The meditative practices are integrated with the physical and technical components in the yearly training program. In the following pages the technique, beginning with the release, is explained in detail. In reality the four parts of the cycle flow into each other as part of a continuous cycle. Each of these phases is simple, integrated, and seamless.

The flow in the stroke cycle can be enhanced by smooth transitions at the entry and release, by even pressure on the blade during the drive, by relaxing on the recovery, and by unhurried movements. With time and practice these specific movements evolve into fine sculling.

The four individual phases of the release, recovery, entry and drive eventually blend into a total stroke cycle where it becomes difficult to separate and make the phases distinct. The cycle becomes one of fluid perpetual motion from the start to the finish of the race. So, there is a system of movement above the seat that includes the trunk, arms, hips and hands, as well as a system below the seat that encompasses the legs and feet.

This integrated technique produces an eight that is sculling the shell. It is extremely helpful if the coaching model is based on a combined approach to training, considering the technical, the mind development and the physical. This is a balanced and thoroughly integrated method.

## Release

For this segment of the stroke, it is extremely critical that the release is performed with high skill. I have attempted to be detailed in describing this complex action. There are three systems involved, the trunk and legs, the forearms and elbows, and the fine movements of the hands and fingers. This important phase represents a simple, whole process, combining five actions into one smooth movement: engaging in quick sequence the hands, wrists, arms, trunk and legs, like a flowing stream. Thus, there are two systems operating, one with the trunk, legs and arms, and a second involving the fine movements of the fingers and handles. In this phase mindfulness is important and emphasized.

A snapshot of the release finds the trunk angled comfortably about 15 degrees past the perpendicular. This angle is maintained with a firm trunk and legs finish. The hands and forearms are level and the thumb knuckles nudge the abdominal wall with a separation of 10-12 inches. The elbows are angled outward away from the mid-line at a comfortable angle. The elbows are positioned in the line of the pull of the hands. The elbows will point downwards if are carried too close to the body as in the old English style. The hands height position corresponds to the length of the upper arm. The hands must be perfectly level.

The position of the upper body facilitates a single movement out of bow. If you had more lay-back it would take two movements to come forward. The wrists are flat as the hands come to the trunk

## Jimmy Joy

moving downward slightly (see Diagram #8) and remain flat as you roll the hands away from the trunk. There follows quickly a slight break in the wrists to feather the blade. However, the wrist action should not dominate the release. The handles are held with the pads, roots of the fingers and fingers shifting to the roots and fingers when the blade is feathered. A good drill is having a light touch on the handles, doing finger sculling.

The blade action is continuous and subtle. The blade is released from the water when it is half out and at a forty-five degree angle (the feathering of the blade is quickly sequenced after the start of the release). This was proven to be the most effective method in the MIT Hydraulic Lab in 1964 by one of my oarsmen, Dr. Dennis Ducik.[35] This can be identified as flat wrist rowing (minimal wrist action) and translates from the sculling into two-handed release action for the rower with both hands performing the identical movements, thus "the roll release." In sweep rowing if you rely on the inside hand only to release, then the thumb acts as a block to the flow of the handle and the wrist breaks severely. The two-handed release fosters flat wrist rowing.

The release forms an elliptical pattern, rather than rectangular. A skilled simulation exercise with the hands is to have one hand mimicking the movement of the oar handle, and the other hand describing the path of the blade; at the same moment, with eyes closed, you visualize the patterns of both actions. An excellent on-water drill for the

---

[35] Is there not a need for more empirical studies on various phases? I think so. - Jimmy

bladework is quarter-slide back-end rowing that allows the athlete to focus entirely on the movements of the release. This is performed in the winter on the ergometer as well.

During the release and follow-through, the function of the trunk and legs shift from being prime movers to stabilizers for the arm and hand actions. The arms work both independently and interdependently with the trunk. The athlete comes out of bow with the initial movement from the elbows. "The elbows come into the body and the elbows go out." This is the coach's mantra, "elbows in, elbows out." Imagine you have a large square box containing a mouth watering thin crust pizza, and you pass the box to share the pie. This simple movement models sculling follow through.

This integrated approach from the bow establishes the balance during the recovery to the entry. The relaxed hands are lowered slightly, the release is a small rounded movement of the wrists and hands, the arms extend, the trunk moves a small distance through the perpendicular position, and the knees rise. The ball and socket joint at the shoulder and the simple hinge joint at the elbow can be employed effectively along with the small muscle covering the elbow, known as the Anconeus. The five movements are executed quickly as one movement to promote smooth flow. These actions set the stage for the timing of the trunk and the seat during the recovery.

## Recovery

The trunk swing is a legacy from the era of the shorter track of Hanlan, but substantially more refined. The trunk remains the important link between the body and the movement of the shell and is the single most important element for developing flow. It should be noted that by lengthening his track to 26 inches, Hanlan made his trunk swing more horizontal and less pronounced.

With the longer track and increased base for his trunk swing, Hanlan's body action changed from a pronounced pendular motion to a subtle, horizontal action still witnessed in modern scullers today. However this "swing" must maintain the connection to the shell movement; this is the basis of flow.

There are two distinct phases to develop this subtle swing consisting of a two season approach. This method involves extensive practice of the well-timed swing in the fall, evolving to an instinctual glide forward in the spring. This is a wonderful transformation from the conscious to the unconscious; as the body glides forward, the shell slides through the water.

During the recovery, the subtle trunk swing is the key to the integration of the body and the shell. There is a fine resonance established between the shell and the body. Visualizing the motion of the cross cut saw is helpful for understanding the body action in the stroke cycle, pull and let go, an almost one to one ratio.

For me, it took miles of concentrated low rate sculling before the strong connection between the body and shell was achieved. It was a wonderful feeling. With time a simple stroke is developed that maximizes the run of the shell and conserves energy at the same time.

The modified trunk swing from the hips carries the seat forward. As trunk swing comes toward the stern let the hands rise from the toes to full reach by un-weighting the hands on the handles. This action by the hands prevents pitching by the shoulders and keeps the blade close to the water. Also, one should allow the heels to rise slightly from the foot stretchers. This removes any stress on the ankles to be flexible. If the heels remain flat on the stretches this tends to "jam" the movement of the trunk and hips. The trunk and seat arrive at the front end together. It is analogous to closing the covers of a good book. The stroke length at the entry comes from leg compression, reaching from the shoulders and hips. The blade is carried on the feather off the water at a height of approximately half the width of the blade. With the knees reaching the armpits is when the entry is quickly, instantly, executed.

The precision of the trunk and seat must be practiced endlessly over the winter in the tanks or on the ergometers. This results in the whole motion having more fluidity and no awkwardness to it. Consequently, this refined hip action is a silent form of kinetic energy that builds as the athlete approaches the entry position.

The athlete should sit lightly on the seat and the trunk should be erect so that he is sitting with proper torso height. Sit on the seat with even pressure on the sit bones of both cheeks.

This is good alignment and posture as outlined earlier. "Sit so lightly that the wind blows under you."

This permits the shell to slide easily under the sculler as he moves naturally towards the stern.

The pressure on the foot stretchers is equal on both feet and the same is true for the lateral pressure on the sculling oarlocks. These three points of contact (seat, feet and oarlocks) maintain the stable, balanced platform that is so essential for an effective entry and drive. It is important to remain symmetrical to the keel at all points in the stroke. The seat posture and relationship of the body to the instrument is similar to the Equestrian and Bike racer. To maintain this strong position the abdominal core has to be thoroughly trained.

Hanlan, with the inception of the sliding seat, quickly mastered this coordinated movement to his advantage with his lively, consistent trunk swing.

He wrote in the *Vancouver World*, Tuesday, April 12, 1898 the following,

> *"When I first took it into my head to follow rowing the boats were inadequate for the purpose.... The shells had a four inch slide. The first time I used it, I noticed a defect somewhere, but I did not locate it for some time. I was out sculling on Toronto bay one day, rowing as hard as I knew, and I began to wonder at the slow rate of progress I was making. I noticed that every time I reached forward for a stroke and put my oars aft that the stern of the boat would sink about four inches in the water. On each occasion I could also feel the seat bump against me, so to speak, checking the movement of my boat to a large extent. I studied the matter for some time and*

*finally concluded that the fault lay in the seat.*

*I went to Mr. Warin the boat builder and asked him to put in another seat with a three inch longer slide. Mr. Warin said that I was a crank and did not know what I wanted. He also added that I was the most ungainly sculler he had ever seen in his life. However, he made the alteration and I resumed my practices on the bay. The seat did not satisfy me, though, and in a short while I went to Mr. Warin again and induced him to add another three inches to the slide on the seat. This proved to be acceptable and I found that the greater freedom I could give my body, the great impetus I could give the boat, and, therefore, attain a faster rate of speed." finally concluded that the fault lay in the seat."*[36]

Seventy years later Ivanov would achieve the same mastery of his upper body coordinated with the movement of the seat on his way to winning three Olympic Gold medals in the single.

This subtle swing provides the simple pattern, the rhythm, and the effortless, efficient, energy saving momentum. The flexibility of the hips and shoulder girdle is very important for developing a well-timed trunk swing. The winter land training should stress flexibility development through yoga and these exercises should be part of the warm-up and cool down during the other training phases. This flexibility, in both the hips and shoulders, leads to an

---

[36] Eventually, Hanlan would lengthen his slide to 26 inches.

increased length of the stroke and to an increase in power.

Hanlan was well aware that the key to stroke efficiency lay in the relationship between the body and the seat. This timing, especially on the recovery, had to be mastered. His inspiration for further improvement came from an ordinary kitchen clock.

He spoke of being attracted by the steady swing of the clock pendulum: "It swung forward and backward, but I could detect, by the closest observation, where the swing ended. That was my cue. I resolved to become a rowing pendulum, if possible, as I realized that the nearest I approached the action of that most useful part of the clock, the better sculler I would become."

This well-timed swing begins in the bow and goes through a transition phase at the entry. It then returns to the bow coordinating with the steady leg drive and fluid arm draw. The individual distances the trunk and shoulders travel must always be the same for maximum effect, similar to the pendular action of a clock. The distance the upper body moves is longer than the seat but arrives at both ends with the seat, to achieve a well timed swing and drive.

An effective drill, both in the shell and on the ergometer, is the set-in at the entry starting from various points on the slide bed. Start at quarter slide and move forward to the entry and simply place the blade in the water quickly. The athlete pauses momentarily, allowing him to assess the timing of the body movements during the recovery and the blade action. Then he resumes his starting position before the next repetition. The athlete can feel if the timing is not quite right. These drills stabilize the "inboard platform" of the body and gunwales during the recovery. The positioning of the blades constitutes the outboard platform and this is addressed in the drive section.

A drill for subtle swing during the drive consists of a single stroke pull through with one pause in the water at entry, and another out of the water at the release. Then repeat the entire sequence.

Every athletic skill has a component with a swing or stride as a major part of the overall movement. The ultimate aim of the various movements engaged is efficiency, smoothness, simplicity and power. So, the stroke looks complete with no loose ends between body, blades and shell; the ingredients are a single unit, a "well-fitted" shoe. It is a "tight" system.

### Diagram 5 - The Trunk Swing

The Trunk Swing: a major key to flow.

The Five Movements of the release & follow through - hands, wrist, arms, trunk, legs - the sequence flows and appears as a single movement.

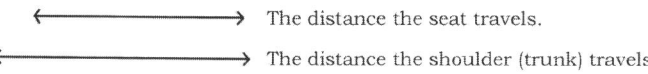

←————————→ The distance the seat travels.
←————————————→ The distance the shoulder (trunk) travels.

Timing - Trunk and Legs are synchronized with the blade work throughout the stroke cycle.

## **Drive**

> *"Hanlan's genius was a superbly efficient stroke – he was the father of the modern technique. He took full advantage of the sliding seat, not only to obtain greater reach but to drive with the large muscles of the legs in a coordinated, fluid motion so that the power of his whole body was marshaled into every stroke."*
>
> Canadian Sports Tribune

The drive integrates the legs, trunk and arms, integrating the power of the components at the entry, creating a strong bond between the body and blade, beginning with a well-timed trunk and legs together at the initial part of the drive (see **Diagram 6)**. The large muscle groups of the upper back, the hip girdle and the legs are integrated for maximum power. The arms are straight at the entry and primed to make the fluid transition from extension to flexion. Hanlan started the drive with the trunk and legs concurrently thus making effective use of his 150 pounds. The more recent approach is using the legs, trunk and arms sequentially. I maintain that the sequencing approach becomes more of an integrated, fluid action with time, practice mileage and racing experience, and looks more like the integrated method. The legs, trunk and arms blend with mileage. After time and mileage the two "methods" begin to look similar.

With the sequencing method the mental focus is on the inboard body movements. With the summation of forces approach the mind focuses on the outboard action of the blade. In preparing for Craftsbury one year, the feel of the blade as I moved towards the release was too light. Eventually I changed the feel of the blades to an even solid pressure throughout the drive. By concentrating on the consistency of the draw of the hands the athlete avoids any yanking or slippage and the acceleration of the handle is natural. This is a definition of "patient" sculling.

If the sculler rigidly sequences the legs, trunk and arms, he is fragmenting his power. An example of this type of sculling being carried to the extreme is the two Canadian scullers, in the 1996 Olympics women and men's singles finals. With proper timing, the sequencing of the movements blend and become more whole much like powerful golf swings.

The golf swing serves as an excellent form of cross training and simulation exercise for the drive and follow through phases. Posture, grip and stance are addressed, similar to the sculling stroke. The athletes should practice the swing from both sides of the body. There are immeasurable benefits for a person's athleticism on learning how to coordinate the weight shift in golf with the swing of the club. The golf swing is an excellent example of integrated power, precision, and smooth, coordinated muscle action. There is much we can learn from watching the professional golfers of posture, rhythm, using the power from the hips and legs and shifting the weight for effect. Similarly in sculling, athletes should learn to effectively shift the body weight from the entry to release. This action is coordinated with the smooth pull of the arms transitioning from extension to flexion. The arm draw is supported by, strong upper back muscles.

The arm action during the drive is one of the most difficult movements to perform properly in a coordinated, fluid movement from extension to flexion. Here is where "you should pull what you can handle" so that you don't lose control of the blade in the water during the drive. It takes a great deal of concentrated drilling and rowing to achieve this coordination. There should be no tugging or yanking of the handle by the sculler.

The movement of the handle should have the appearance of steady smoothness from the entry to the release. The arm action is assisted with the strong involvement of the large muscle groups of the upper back. This insures that the transition from extension of the arms to flexion is a fluid and subtle. Recently, I viewed a men's quad at the Lucerne World Cup regatta and observed a lack of fluidity in their arm transitions during the drive phase. They were yanking the handle, which is not efficient for producing power. On the other hand, as I watched Katrin Ruchow, the women's sculler from Germany in the 2004 Olympics, I could see she was extremely fluid and relaxed with her arm draw.

Hanlan's technique for beginning the drive was replicated by his good friends, Jim Ten Eyck, and Jim's son Ned, of Syracuse. All three were small men who effectively applied their sparse bodyweight. Eventually, the three would be considered among the finest scullers in rowing history. Their size, efficiency and power were comparable to today's modern golfers.

The initiation of the drives integrates the power of the shoulders, arms and the legs and carries this wholeness throughout the drive. This coordination of the body is referred to as the "Yale fixed seat" principle or summation of forces. Looking at old pictures in the Yale Tanks in New Haven, I pondered how they rowed with a fixed seat and came up with three methods: the athletes simply pulled with the arms; or they used a trunk swing followed by an arm draw; or, and I thought this was the most effective way, they coordinated the trunk and arms. The coach can demonstrate this method from a standing stationary position that is analogous to the fixed seat rowing by walking backwards drawing the arms to the body. This is reminiscent of the fixed seat principle applied to the sliding seat. The drive is effective if you do not try to pull too hard and maintain even pressure on the handles throughout the movement. The shoulders remain level during the drive phase minimizing the trunk movement from the hips.

**Diagram 6 - The Fixed Seat Principle**

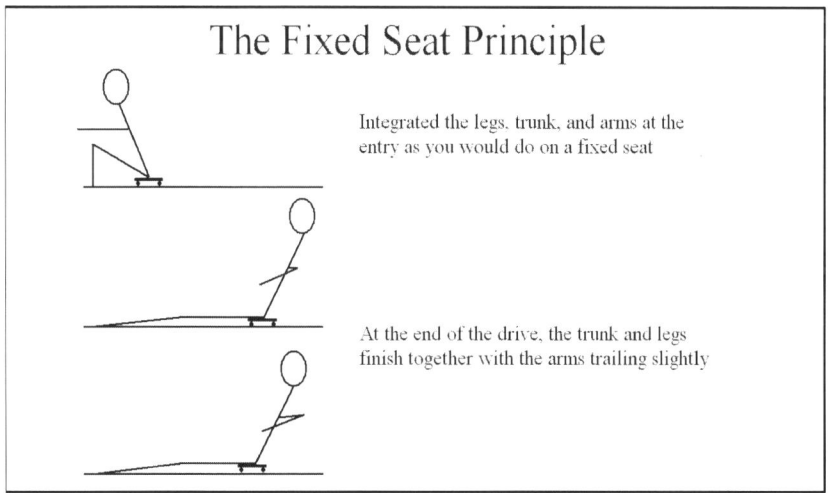

Olympic medalist Carly Geer stresses the movement at the entry coordinates the hands pulling with the knees moving downward. This focused concentration develops a wonderfully coordinated draw of the arms throughout the length of drive integrated with the legs, trunk and blade forming a "tight" system with no loose ends.

## Diagram 7 - The Coordinated Hand and Knee Action During the Initial Part of the Drive

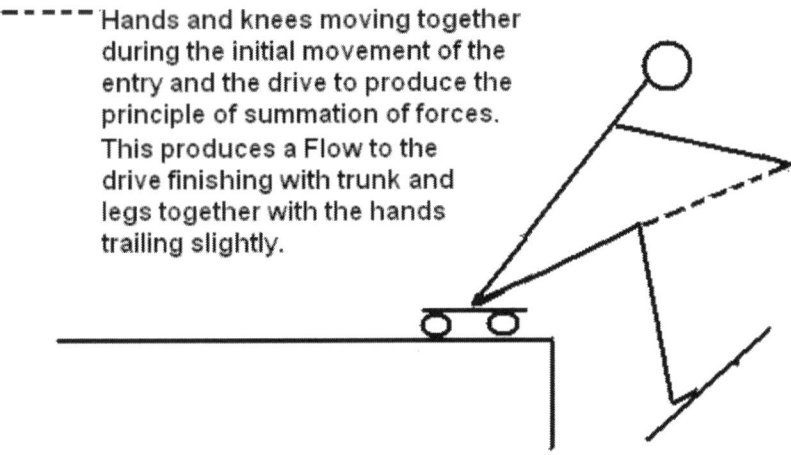

Hands and knees moving together during the initial movement of the entry and the drive to produce the principle of summation of forces. This produces a Flow to the drive finishing with trunk and legs together with the hands trailing slightly.

The coordination of the shoulders and the arms is carried through the length of the track by the steady leg pressure from the balls of the feet.
The athlete should feel the sequential activation of the various muscle groups in the legs from toes, to lower legs to quads and hamstrings. The legs move inward to the mid-line as the legs go down. This action produces a flow to the body, creating a one-piece drive. It is extremely important to visualize the integration of each of these major segments with the blade work during the drive and recovery.

It is important to visualize towards the end of the stroke that the bow deck remains level as sculler or crew shift their weight to the bow as the drive phase finishes and the release is executed. So the sculler "visualizes up" as he moves towards the bow- the hands, head, torso and shoulders.

Relaxation in the body movements during the drive will allow the full expression of the athlete's power. Straining or tightening creates the opposite, by reducing it. You can see evidence of relaxation in the faces of sprinters at the finish of the 100-meter dash. Our crews and scullers should display this placid demeanor. Old photos of Hanlan, Pearce and Kelly Sr. certainly display this quality. It is also important that at higher skill levels there develops the correct balance between relaxation and inhibition. When the athlete consciously inhibits some specific muscle action he is engaged in economy of motion and this is positive.

Some outstanding examples of this accurate circumscribed swing in modern scullers are Vyacheslav Ivanov in the late 1950s and early 1960s, along with Thomas Lange in 1988, Peter Haining in 1994 and Zeno Müller and Katerina Karsten in 1996. Both Lange and Ivanov in particular, exemplify the flow of Hanlan. The parameters to their stroke cycles were clear and consistent leading to a beautiful rhythm from the start to the finish of the race.

Haining, in winning the world championship in 1994, exclaimed after the race, "I felt like a runaway freight train." This is a perfect example of Flow.

The important item that is usually neglected during these phases is the posture of the feet and the legs. The leg drive comes from the "balls of the feet" with the heels slightly raised. The legs are evenly, symmetrically splayed one to one and a half hand-widths apart and are in a firm solid position to perform the seated lifting movement of the drive. There should be no wobbly legs. It is important to develop exactness, precision and integration of these movements so that there is flow and effortlessness. This is an example of a highly integrated action of the legs, arms, and trunk.

An excellent drill for the drive is the single stroke pull through, starting from a stationary full slide position, drawing to the release finishing trunk and legs together, pausing momentarily before resuming the entry position for another single stroke pull. Position the blade in the water, pause, and then do another steady pull to the finish. This drill isolates a part of the stroke with the emphasis on focused attention to detail.

For bladework placement accuracy and control, an important drill is to scull with a blade at three quarter covered, to half covered, to quarter covered. This extra benefit of this drill is that the athlete has to move more slowly.

## Diagram 8 - Covering the Blade Partially for Accuracy and Control

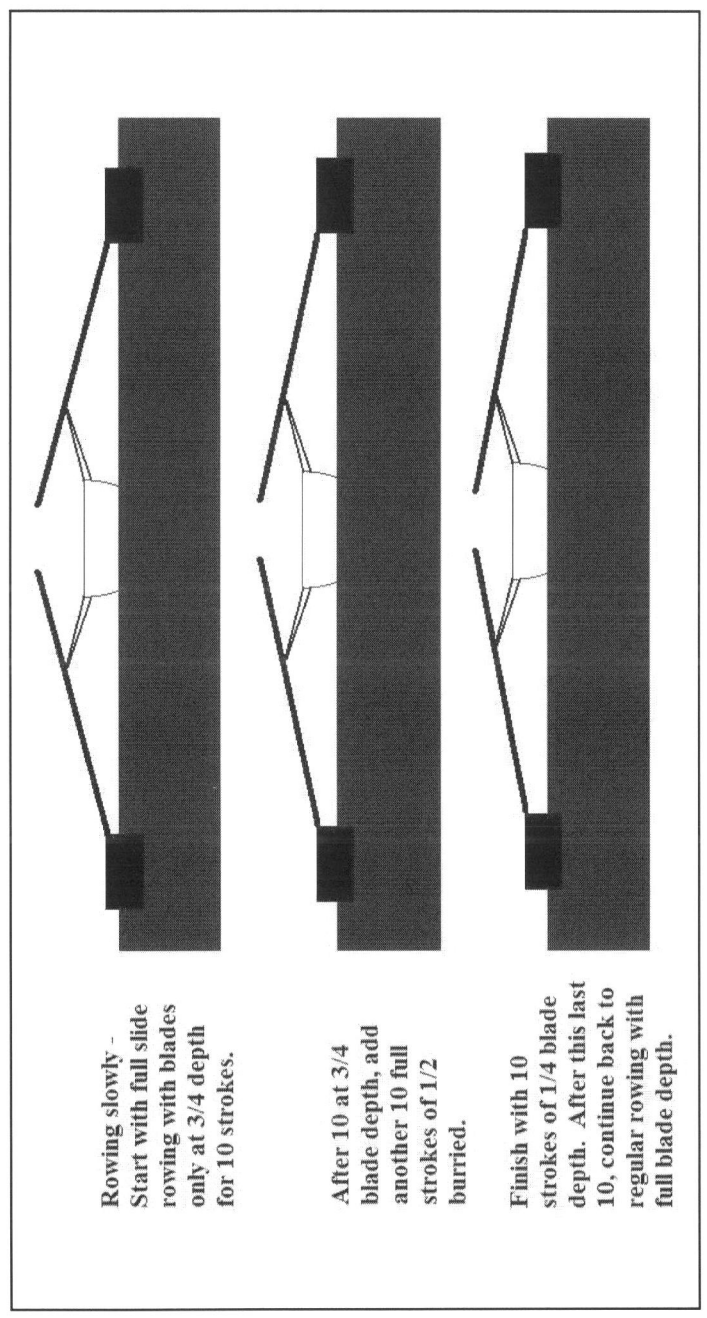

Rowing slowly - Start with full slide rowing with blades only at 3/4 depth for 10 strokes.

After 10 at 3/4 blade depth, add another 10 full strokes of 1/2 burried.

Finish with 10 strokes of 1/4 blade depth. After this last 10, continue back to regular rowing with full blade depth.

A good lead up to this drill is to do set-ins at

You can continue this work by rowing at three quarter slide with a three quarter covered blade, at half slide with a half covered blade and at quarter slide with a quarter covered blade.

## Diagram 9 - Stationary Drill for Blade Depth

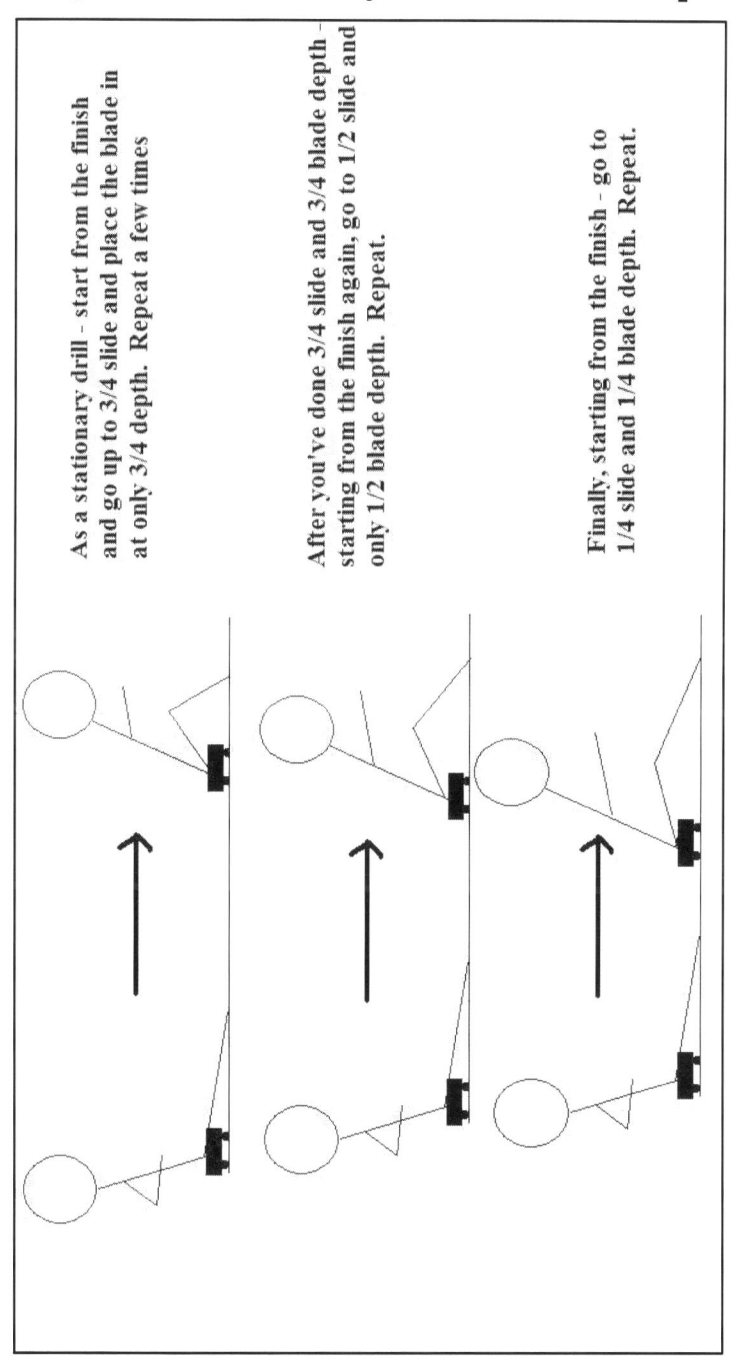

These drills help in stabilizing the "outboard platform" of the blade position in the water. The eye can detect the stability of the inboard platform but usually not the "outboard platform" of the blade accuracy in the water. The sculling drill is much more difficult than the set-in drill. It can be viewed as an active concentration similar to the walking meditation of the Buddhists. The sculler must slow down and focus intently on the accuracy of blade work.

Quick release, effective subtle swing, quick entry, the relaxed, accurate, refined movements of the hands and an integrated drive with precise blade placement, produce an aggressive stroke and a lively shell run. As stated earlier, when properly executed, the shell should slide through the water.

The first time that I witnessed this quality in an International crew was in 1976 in St. Catharines before the Montreal Olympics. I watched Bob Janousek's Great Britain eight in practice. The shell was extremely lively and slid continuously with each stroke.

## Entry

From the release the hands working with the trunk move downward slightly and are carried forward to the entry position with a slight pressure on the oar handle. The hands rise to full reach over the feet, as weight shifts from the handle to blade, allowing it to drop easily into the water. The hands move upwards from the toes to full reach preventing the shoulders from pitching forward. With the knees swinging into the armpits, this position is an immediate indicator for the quick execution of the entry. The trunk is straight but not rigid with the head erect looking ahead over the stern. The hands are perfectly level at the entry. The easy, relaxed reach is from the shoulders, hips and legs. The legs are placed with lower leg at right angles to the gunwale. When the body is at full reach, the blade is buried. The athlete observes the stern deck remaining level with a continuous movement of the hull. This is the shell sliding.

There are two unconventional entry methods for sculling. The "pivot" or intermediate method is a quickly sequenced movement of the blade. With this approach the blade quickly pivots, drops and pulls in one continuous action. The blade is carried close to the water because the blade is pivoted at the midline; the forward or bow edge of the blade is brought towards the stern with the pivot action and as the blade is being pivoted, it is moving downwards towards the water. Crews will unconsciously employ this method when they do the "touching up" exercise to turn the shell. Now the trick is to do it consciously on the move at a specific point in the stroke cycle. This is "lower edge rowing" and it is an excellent method for the college crew. Using the hands to demonstrate or simulate the pivoting action is very helpful.

  The second method is the Fitzpatrick or the old sculling catch, in which the blade simply disappears.[37] It is similar to the entry used by the old professionals like Hanlan. It is the more difficult of the two to master. It involves a significant shift in our traditional thinking. This second method has been lost over the past 50 years. The last successful athlete to use this entry was Gold Medalist Conn Findlay of the USA. The position of the blade moves quickly from the horizontal slightly above the water to the vertical in the water. This is the inverse action to the release. It angles into the water. I recall feeling the blade shift from a slightly over-squared position in the water to the squared or perpendicular placement. You didn't simply rely on the external pitch of the rigging. You had your own internal pitch mechanism where through the feel of your hands you were connected to the blade in the water.

  Both methods take the water instantly with a strong feeling of the load on the blade in the shoulder girdle. This is a positive indicator of a good entry. Consequently, along with the legs, the strength in the large shoulder muscles in the upper back must be developed.

  At the end of the recovery, when the knees are in the armpits, the knuckles of the hands rise quickly followed by a drawing of the hands towards the bow

---

[37] At Wesleyan in 1976, this is how students described it in seeing a demonstration of the entry.

and a raising of the wrists. On land again simulate these small hand actions at the entry. Practice the rhythmic quality of the movement of the hand and knuckle by simulating the action of moving the knuckles up slightly followed by a draw of the hand towards the body with the wrists rising to the level or flat position. This exercise with the hands is a miniature "rocking chair" motion. Observing the hand action you can see the flow of the movement.

During this quick sequence the blade is allowed to drop into the water in a slightly over-squared position. The sculler "lets" the blade drop into the water by relaxing the grip and the downward pressure on the scull handles. This allows the blade to have a continuous movement because the blade is not squared above the water and then set into the water. The sculler's entry is unconventional because there is no preparation phase. Consequently, there is no pause in the blade moving from the horizontal to the vertical position in the water. This unchecked hand action contributes significantly to the shell sliding through the water.

**Diagram 10 - The Continuous Movement of the Blade & Handle**[38]

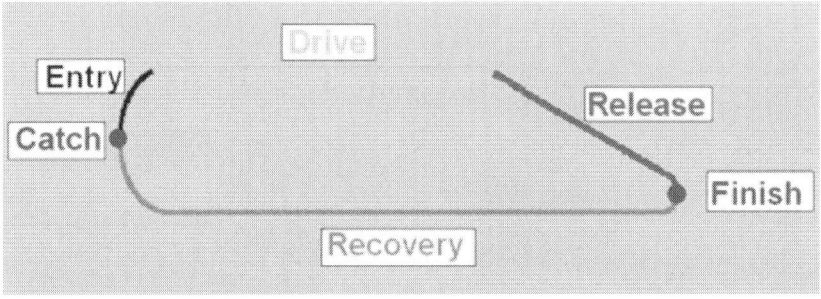

---

[38] Nolte, Volker. September, 2007. (Note: There is no mention of preparation in this diagram)

Skillful use of the hands was demonstrated by the Pearce by employing only his fingers to enter and release the blade from the water keeping his wrists consistently in the flat position.[39] This had to be very economical and quick.

This instinctive, intuitive and reflexive sculling entry is similar to the methods of Ned Hanlan and of old professional watermen. It is a good example of superb sculling athleticism.

Two music lovers reminded me of the piano playing analogy for the flat wrists and light fingers, historian friend Marvin Bram and Mark Evans, a Gold Medalist in the Men's 1984 Olympic Eight. Recently, Marvin recounted to me the hand action of the eminent Vladimir Horowitz, with his "fast-wrist" pianism of light, fast hands and fingers. Mark, in a conversation in 1987 after a practice, took me aside at the completion of my talk on flow to a group of athletes and related the flat wrists and light finger action in rowing to his own piano playing. He added that his power came from his Hara as he pointed to and touched his stomach. He was in touch with his inner self.

Observing the hands of instrumentalists whether playing the cello, violin or piano is always a particular pleasure. There is agility, dexterity, rhythm, to flow of the fingers and a lightness of touch. Recently, in enjoying a concert of five instrumentalists, I was struck by the parallels between the integration involving the string quintet and an eight.

---

[39] According to sculling coach Robert Fitzpatrick from a conversation in 1955.

Similar to Hanlan's "sharp and quick entry" the blade almost feels like it is programmed to go unerringly to blade depth and cup the water. The athlete feels immediately the power application and the initial responsiveness of the shell.

The positioning of the blade at a depth of the blade width results in the Bernoulli Effect, where there are high and low pressure areas on each side of the blade face, and where the blade "cups" the water creating a smooth "wall of water" in front and a slight depression behind. If the blade is too deep or too shallow you cannot achieve this effect. This effect can be easily demonstrated at the dockside and it should be part of the young athlete's initiation to the sport, not necessarily during the first practice but in the first few months.

This firm blade action of gripping the water assists with integrating the body segments during the drive phase. It feels as though the body is suspended by the firm grip of the blades on the water. Even pressure on the blade, integrated with the body movements of the trunk, legs, and arms, combined with consistency in the stroke length, develops the elusive rhythm of the sculler. By focusing on even pressure you don't have to worry about accelerating the handle during the drive. The handle has to accelerate to feel the even pressure.

So, the important question is, from what position is the blade dropped? Is it from the square or horizontal? If you scrutinize old photos of famous scullers you will never see the blades squared above the water. The movement of the entry is executed too quickly. The blades are either feathered or in the entry position. A deeper visualization is the key to a good entry because you cannot see the blades at this point in the cycle.

Einstein's maxim is helpful with the entry when he states, "The imagination is more important than knowledge." You have to able to visualize the pattern of placing the blade in the water at full extension. It helps with the visualization of the movement if you have the athletes describe the action employing their hands as the blades (see the drill below). It is also helpful to concentrate on observing the movement of the hands in front of you at the entry. There is a definite flow action to the movement of the fingers and wrists.

The East German literature characterized the entry in this way: "The crucial prerequisite for fast entry is a late and quick squaring of blades with the blades carried close to the water." Recently, biomechanics expert Valery Kleshnev stated, "Rapid force development at the catch and longer maintenance at the finish of the drive must be emphasized instead of applying highest peak force in the middle of the drive." I suggest that the quick blade and hand action lead directly to quick force application. This entry creates an immediate feeling of shell responsiveness that remains with you throughout your life in a single. This is a similar feeling of Hanlan's "single being drawn by a string."

You will want to avoid square blade rowing until the lower edge rowing is firmly established. It is a high skill drill for balance not for bladework. The finish form of your entry or the release is not similar to square blade rowing. It is more elliptical where the square blades are rectangular. The lower edge continuous rowing is the key ingredient for maintaining flow. Too much square blade rowing reinforces having the blade squared above the water in a pause mode. Ideally the lower edge must move down continuously towards the water. During the recovery the blade is positioned close to the water. The positioning of the blade and the entry action insures a solid and instant transfer of power. Minimize the instruction to allow the athlete to flow with the oar handle. By minimizing the instruction, the entry becomes more intuitive and reflexive. Eventually this is the quality that you are seeking in the whole stroke cycle. Years ago a Yale oarsman, Al Minier, when asked how he achieved his beautiful entry simply responded, "I let the hands follow the oar handle."[40] His approach to the entry was the first method described earlier. His action was instinctive.

The DDR Landvoight Twins in the late 1970s were masters of moving a square blade down and into the water in one smooth uninterrupted movement. Observing Olympic Champion Matthew Pinsent at the Seville Training camp in 2001 showed that he did not possess the same skill level as the twins. He was constantly rowing with a slight pause in the blade action above the water before the entry. He needed to do more single sided rowing so that he could observe his own blade pattern at the entry to make it more continuous. Most scullers and crews that employ the square blade drill pause above the water before entering. To reduce this tendency square blade rowing should be minimized and used for economy and balance by monitoring the blade height off the water on the recovery and how much the hands have to be lowered at the release.

---

[40] Conversation with Al Minier, Yale '70, in 1970.

One final point on the entry is that the blade enters the water at a point where the arc is not "pinching" the boat. Thus the blade moves towards the stern rather than pushing away from the sides of the shell. Proper rigging assures that this type of blade action occurs.

Examples of effective drills for the entry include the "touching up" drill, dropping the blade in vertically from a stationary position. The hands and brain must know the pattern of the blade. The "set-ins" at the entry from three quarter, half, quarter, and zero slide are good practice for the continuous bladework. Another effective drill is to sit at full reach and practice dropping the blade into the water from the horizontal position. The blade will have more flow once the athlete begins to row continuously. The standard drill for the entry is quarter slide front end continuous sculling. The drill performed accurately has the sculler releasing in front of the knees.

Both the entry and release movements can be simulated effectively using the hands as blades. It is a revealing drill for how the athlete pictures the two movements.

## Summary

*...my experience may one day be recognized as a signpost directing the explorer to a country hitherto "undiscovered," and one which offers unlimited opportunity for fruitful research to the patient and observant pioneer.*
F. Matthias Alexander

My passion to understand and promote the phenomenon known as flow has been a lifelong pursuit. I recall observing from an early age the fluid, economic swings and movements of the great athletes of the day. Maybe being an undersized athlete in most of my sporting activities sparked my interest and study of flow. It seemed obvious to me efficiency of movement was the equalizer, and the way to achieve it was through flow. I recognized early on that training for flow was very much a part of my commitment to cultivating the mind as well as the body.

The flow of the body and its accompanying instruments, the oar and shell, are the external manifestations of internal harmony, balance, and rhythm. Then it is critical that the coach recognizes "the sculler's organism as a unity where the working of any of the parts is affected by the working of the whole."[41] Smooth action in each part of the movement will eventually result in fluidity in the whole stroke cycle. The teaching emphasis is clearly on the means rather than the end. End gaining mentally almost insures stiffness and failure. This principle also applies equally to the lone sculler, to a crew and to the coach. They are all part of a dedicated systematic approach for the evolution of the organism and the resulting effortless technique.

F. Matthias Alexander, the great expert on movement recognized that the human mind and body were an inseparable whole. The sculler must view the mind, body and the equipment as a whole.

The coach himself leads flow by example, by instilling all aspects of his coaching with consistent transparent fluidity. The greater the flow of the coach, the more effective he becomes at fostering this quality in his athletes. Once the athlete understands and commits to this objective, the coach has at last become a consummate choreographer and the sculler a more complete athlete.

Total integration of mind, body, emotions, and spirit advances the development of this smooth movement of unconscious flow. The coach attempts to produce this level of athleticism in his oarspeople through a comprehensive training program.

Sculling is a rare opportunity to experience a more integrated life. It unifies our consciousness and spirit, which when combined with our knowledge of science and art, inspires us to reach a fuller understanding of ourselves.

---

[41] F. Matthias Alexander, *The Resurrection of the Body* (New York, NY: University Books, 1969).

For integration to occur, openness by the coach and the athlete is necessary to permit the multiple layers of our inner world to surface and become part of our awareness. Integration implies not only the internal and external and the rational and intuitive, but also the art and science of the experience. It is holistic in considering a broad range of information from various disciplines.

The coach is working with the athlete's essential self, human nature in the broadest sense - mind, body, spirit development, corresponding to the technical, physical and mental aspects of training. With this approach, the learning process is enjoyable and there is a high degree of self-realization by the student and the teacher. The exploration of your limits and personal growth is stressed in contrast to a more competitive model. With the full development over the years of each of these aspects of 'fitness', the basic bodily movements are easier to perform, appear unhurried, and relaxed. This approach allows the athlete a greater range of development, a more relaxed motion, and creates an enjoyable learning environment. The sport remains childlike, playful, and the athlete's self becomes more expansive; he feels his growth beyond the boundaries of his own skin.

In understanding the athlete, the coach reaches an understanding of his own self. The virtues of the self include stillness rather than movement; silence in place of speech; being rather than becoming; and, the importance of inner essence over outer substance. With this type of philosophy, the learning process, especially in training for smooth technique, cannot be hurried.

Outstanding coaches personify this expansiveness of mind by living their philosophy. Their being and doing, thinking and action are one as the coach attempts to integrate mind, matter, and spirit. This is the tradition of the early philosophers from antiquity who were healers and tutors, not just abstract thinkers. They lived their philosophies. With this approach, his boat-side manner can function effectively as his knowledge is easily conveyed and understood by the athlete. The athletes develop into an invaluable source of information for the coach.

As stated earlier, Ned Hanlan was fortunate to have the quiet setting of Toronto Island Lagoon for his home and practice site. One can only imagine the countless miles and hours spent by this man in the relative seclusion of this placid waterway. Here he could approach his sculling like an artist and elementary scientist with the body, shell and water as his vehicle to transform himself into the master waterman and sculler. Probably, he is the apotheosis of sculling skill, and comprehensive training. His advice is still relevant:

> *The science of sculling is almost a difficult one to master, and requires a number of years experience, combined with a steady application and constant thought to arrive at any degree of perfection...Those who aspire to prominence and fame in this great branch of sport place too much reliance on their physical strength, allowing the scientific principles to escape them to a large extent. An experience of 24 years devoted to the study of rowing has taught me that mere endurance and brute strength do not make the successful oarsman.... In*

*other words, the man must use his head as well as his physical gifts.*

There were so many similar moments for me in my life and in my athletics when I have felt completely at home in this world of athletic flow whether it be walking, jogging, swimming, skating, sculling, driving an automobile, or simply looking at the ocean. I felt integrated with my environment in a completely enmeshed state. There were no boundaries separating me from the natural world. This is a finer aspect of our being that can be experienced throughout our life. The eminent physicist Erwin Schrodinger wrote succinctly, "Becoming is conscious, being unconscious."

The present athletes who follow Hanlan using the shell as a vehicle, strive to enhance, enlighten and expand Being. The shell and sculling are the touchstones and I still remember the feeling of the shell and trunk integrated. There was an immediate feel of the shell gliding under me.

> *We may be highly educated, but if we are without a deep integration of thought and feeling, our lives are incomplete, contradictory, and torn with many fears; as long as education does not cultivate an integrated outlook on life, it has little significance.*[42]

Just as modern technology will never replace the experience of human interaction with uniqueness of the river, lake, and in some cases ocean. So too the

---

[42] J. Krishnamurti, *Education and the Significance of Life* (New York, NY: Harper, 1953).

beauty of sculling, with its ability to connect our inner wildness with the natural world, cannot be replicated by science or technology. Sculling provides a unique opportunity to dig deep in the quarry of timelessness and wisdom to unearth the wonderful nuggets found in our inner consciousness. This is the path towards wholeness and integration. This was and remains the ultimate spirit of the diminutive Hanlan. May we ever remember his message.

## **Postscript**

The sculling entry was a wonderful gift from the old master, Bob Fitzpatrick. During my years at the St. Catharines Rowing Club other athletes would ask about the method for achieving such an excellent entry. Fitz, as with many of the coaches at that time, was quite secretive, "tell no one nothing." His secret was safe with me because the entry was a mystery to me, and it was only through careful self-study using Fitz's coaching notes and trial that I subsequently came to understand the intricacies and efficiency of this entry.

Little did I realize the pain that knowledge of this method would cause me in subsequent years. After college when I started coaching at a local high school in St. Catharines I experienced my first conflict. The crew in the fall of 1961 was quite good, defeating local high schools and colleges. In early-spring a representative from the local rowing club visited the school and informed the principal that I was no longer the coach. The primary reason was the mysterious method of the entry.

This situation only acerbated my painful experience with sculling. During my competitive years Fitzpatrick and myself were ostracized from the club because of his methods. Fitz was relegated to an isolated spot on the banks of the old Welland Canal and was never allowed to coach from a launch.

In 1964 I went to MIT as the Freshman coach. Early in the following spring the crew was going in the opposite direction from Harvard freshmen on the Charles. The Harvard coach took a good and prolonged look at my crews. He continued to look until his crews rounded the bend at the Cambridge boathouse. I can only assume that he was observing the unorthodox entry. The MIT Head Coach and the Harvard staff were in close communication. The following day, he instructed me to change the crew's entry. His crews rowed with their blades about a foot off the water before the entry whereas my crews were inches. This was my second extreme shock in less than three years and I never really recovered until this year.

In subsequent years I would employ a modified version of the sculling entry described in this book. At Craftsbury I avoided volunteering for teaching the entry and even felt great fear of being asked to do this particular part of the curriculum. However it was also at Craftsbury that Peter Orlick one of the coaches remarked, "you have a beautiful entry." During this same period at Wesleyan I asked some of the better athletes to describe what they were seeing with my sculling. They responded. that the blade simply disappears at the entry, "we see it and then we don't see it."

Now with the completion of this little book with its detailed account of the entry, I feel a great release and yet a little disappointment that I was not able to coach this entry.

Over the years it has been painful to observe crews at all levels from high school to International levels pause with the blades above the water before the entry. Neil Campbell's crews were an exception as they employed the modified approach. My hope that this book will inspire people to follow the lineage of Hanlan, the Ten Ecycks, Kelly and the incomparable

Pearce by trying to master this excellent sculling entry.

## **By Way of Thanks**

Most of the information in this book originated from conference presentations, clinics, various editions of this work, and conversations that took place over the last twelve years. I am grateful to the many wonderful people and locations that discussed the concepts surrounding Flow. It has been my primary preoccupation in a lifetime of sport and many coaches and academics have influenced my thinking. This has been truly an integrated approach in formulating these books.

The book is dedicated to my parents. My father's skill as an athlete of Flow did not go unnoticed in my early years in the sport. My parents were always quietly supportive of my quest to experience and understand the concept through the wonderful coaching of Bob Fitzpatrick.

My daughters Christina, Kathleen, Alicia, and my wife Cecilia have always provided me with an encouragement and their thoughts on reading the manuscript.

I am very appreciative of Nich Lee Parker for his formatting and extensive efforts in getting this book published. Nich is continuing the format that he began with The Mind's Eye. He has been a tremendous supporter and contributor to my writing for the past three years.

I am most grateful and thrilled that an ex-Yale oarsman Al Minier of 40 years ago has made thorough reads and extensive contributions to this book.

Bob Blase an ex-Navy rower has earned my appreciation for his comments and enthusiastic support for this book and *The Mind's Eye*. He has used the lessons contained with his own scullers.

Greg Yurkow and Mike Wagner have helped considerably with the various diagrams. Greg has done some unique things in devising the diagrams for the drive and blade placement. Mike has updated the diagram for the recovery.

Kit Casey has again done a magnificent job with the art work on the cover. She certainly has a flair for the material from her involvement in our beautiful sport.

My special gratitude goes to Ric Ricci for sharing his knowledgeable insights on this subject in his very complimentary introduction. Ric is enjoying coaching and personal sculling success exploring and utilizing the concepts contained in the book. With our innumerable discussions over the years he has been a wonderful friend and listener.

Also, I am humbled by Larry Gluckman's glowing review of the book. He has certainly captured and embraced the spirt of Hanlan in his successful coaching career.

Finally, I am eternally appreciative of the many hours that Beth Zwecher has logged in her role as editor. She has provided insights, wisdom, and solid direction in her edits from her many reads, concrete suggestions, and rewrites of passages from the manuscript. She has been a wonderful co-worker and friend on so many levels with this project. She has been extremely patient over this long process of writing and rewriting. Her warmth, intelligence and skill is evident in her sensitive and thoughtful foreword to the book.

I consider this book not the final word on this subject but rather a nice spring board for future research and study of a great Canadian sculler and flow master in the incomparable Ned Hanlan.

# Bibliography

Alexander, F. Matthias. *The Resurrection of the Body.* New York, NY: University Books, 1969.

Araton, Harvey. "Nowitski Moment Is a Footnote Back Home." *New York Times*, June 6, 2006 2006.

Bannister, Roger. *The Four-Minute Mile.* New York: Lyons & Burford, 1989.

Consentino, Frank. "Ned Hanlan— Canada's Premier Oarsman: A Case Study in 19th Century Professionalism." University of Western Ontario, 1974.

Csikszentmihalyi, Mihaly. *Flow: The Psychology of Optimal Experience.* New York, NY: Harper & Row, 1990.

Csikszentmihalyi, Mihaly. "Play and Intrinsic Rewards." *Journal of Humanistic Psychology* 15, no. 3 (1975).

Feuerstein, Georg. *Structures of Consciousness: The Genius of Jean Gebser - an Introduction and Critique.* Lower Lake, CA: Integral Publishing, 1987.

Hanlan, Ned. "The Oar." *Vancouver World*, April 12 1898.

Herrigel, Eugen. *Zen in the Art of Archery.* New York, NY: Vintage Books, 1989.

Joy, Jimmy. "The Art of Sculling." In *NAAO (Now USRA) Annual Meeting.* Syracuse, NY, 1978.

Joy, Jimmy. *The Mind's Eye: Mental Training for the Coach.* New York: Joy of Sculling, 2002.

Kelley, R.F. *American Rowing: Its Background and Traditions*: G. P. Putnam's sons, 1932.

Krishnamurti, J. *Education and the Significance of Life.* New York, NY: Harper, 1953.

Lings, Martin. *Ancient Beliefs & Modern Superstitions.* Revised ed. London: Archetype, 2001.

Ming, Shi. *Mind over Matter: Higher Martial Arts.* Berkeley, CA: North Atlantic Books, 1994.

Mitchell, Stephen. *Tao Te Ching.* New York, NY: Harper, 1988.

Page, Geoffrey. *Coaching for Rowing.* London,: Museum Press, 1963.

Ralston, Peter. *Cheng Hsin : The Principles of Effortless Power*. 2nd ed. Berkeley, Calif.: North Atlantic Books, 1999.

Siegel, Daniel J. *The Mindful Brain : Reflection and Attunement in the Cultivation of Well-Being*. 1st ed. New York: W.W. Norton, 2007.

Suzuki, Shunryu, and Trudy Dixon. *Zen Mind, Beginner's Mind*. 1st ed. New York, NY: Weatherhill, 1970.

West, Thomas J. *Ned Hanlan*.

Wilber, Ken. *The Collected Works of Ken Wilber*. Boston, MA: Shambhala, 1999.

Wilber, Ken. *Integral Psychology: Consciousness, Spirit, Psychology, Therapy*. Boston, MA: Shambhala, 2000.

Wilmarth, Art, Corrospondence on "Sliding" Characteristic of Swimmers.

Printed in Dunstable, United Kingdom